CREATE YOUR FINANCIAL PLAN

WITHOUT THE LONG HOURS OR SLEEPLESS NIGHTS

RYAN INMAN, MBA
WITH TAYLOR INMAN, M.D.

Financial Residency
Create Your Financial Plan Without the Long Hours or Sleepless Nights

Hardcover ISBN: 978-1-61206-199-3
Softcover ISBN: 978-1-61206-197-9
eBook ISBN: 978-1-61206-200-6
PDF eBook ISBN: 978-1-61206-198-6
Audiobook ISBN: 978-1-61206-201-3

Interior and Cover Design by: Fusion Creative Works, FusionCW.com
Cover Design Credit: Jonathan Herzog
Lead Editor: Megan Chambers

For more information, visit FinancialResidency.com

To purchase this book at discounted prices, go to AlohaPublishing.com or email alohapublishing@gmail.com

Published by

AlohaPublishing.com
Printed in the United States of America

To the *Financial Residency* community

CONTENTS

This book will help you create a financial life plan that will start you on the right path for not only your ideal finances but your ideal life. We will look at what you want your life to be like and how to put your dollars where they will best enable you to achieve that ideal life.

To make this as easy as possible, I created a free course to lead you through this process that includes more explanations, downloadable forms, and additional resources.

Join this course right now at financialresidency.com/freecourse so you have these resources available as you work through the book.

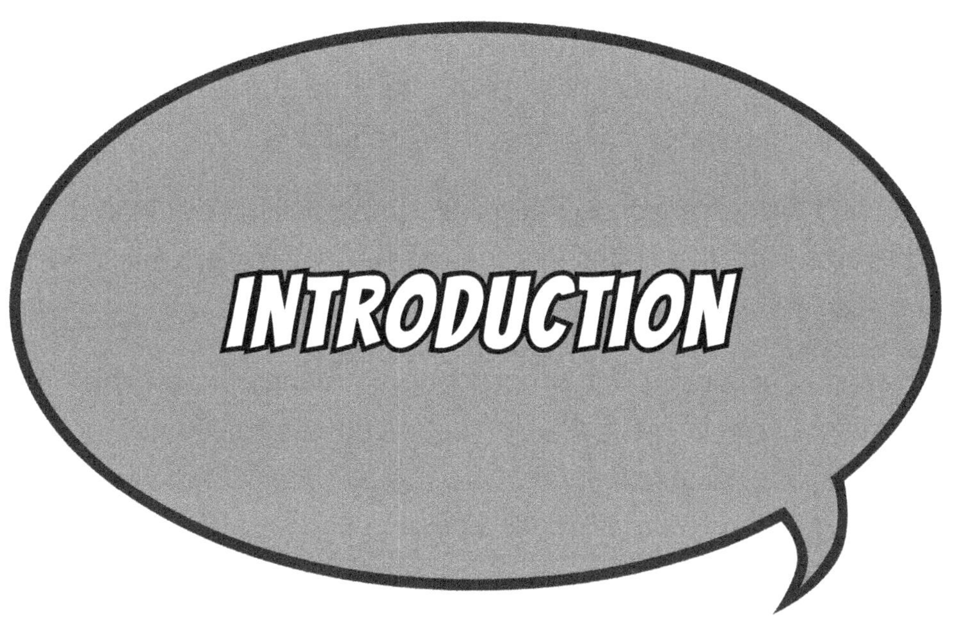

INTRODUCTION

As a physician or physician's spouse, you can create your ideal life. While this book is a guide to financial planning, it is also meant to empower you to think about your future in order to reduce financial stress. Our goal as a physician family is to help you gain freedom with your money and be economically savvy.

I'm Taylor Inman, pediatric pulmonologist and wife of Ryan Inman. We wrote this book to help you create your own financial plan without the long hours and sleepless nights. Ryan is the founder of Physician Wealth Services and host of the *Financial Residency* podcast. His life goal is to help physicians understand their personal finances to gain financial freedom and let their money work for them. Physicians have a late start in building personal wealth and most have mountains of debt. Making good financial decisions early on can set physicians up for financial independence and success.

A financial plan is the foundation upon which you will build your financial life. It will help guide you during the good and bad times, ups and downs of the market, job changes, and financial setbacks.

It's critical to build a financial plan that is unique to you and your family. After all, personal finance is personal.

This book will allow you to build a customized financial plan. It will equip you with the necessary knowledge to protect your income and live your version of your best life.

Creating a financial plan is not all about money, budgeting, and investing. Those things will help you build financial independence, but if you are not sure what you are building wealth for, what is the point of working so hard? That's why your financial plan must focus on your individual goals.

Your goals may change over time, but this book will help you identify and discuss them so you can create a plan that focuses on what makes you happiest. Anything is possible; you just need to plan for it. If your goal is to take a year off work and live on a boat while you travel the world, go for it. Calculate the cost, start saving, and work it into your financial plan. Of course you'll have to make some sacrifices, but working toward a purpose—your goals—helps you avoid burnout. You'll also come to better understand how the money you make can affect your overall happiness.

It is never too early to start thinking about your goals and ideal life. Ryan and I made some choices during my residency and fellowship that changed the trajectory of our lives and set us up for financial independence much sooner than we had initially anticipated. The plan you create as you go through this book will help you avoid costly financial mishaps. You can become financially independent sooner than you thought possible.

As a physician, you didn't get into medicine to become rich, but the financial deck is stacked against you as you begin your career. Physicians tend to take on massive student debt, don't save or invest until their early 30s, and don't receive any financial education. To top it off, the financial industry puts a target on your back knowing you have a lack of financial education and a large income.

Thankfully, you can avoid the pitfalls that many physicians fall into by crafting a financial plan that focuses on what's important to you. You'll begin by identifying your life goals and the things that bring you joy so you can prioritize your spending.

Many physicians fall into the trap of lifestyle inflation and end up spending their money on fancy houses, cars, clothing, and vacations, until they have little left over for other things that truly matter to them. While you can live that way, you may have to work longer because you won't have enough saved for your priorities. Time is your most precious commodity, and we want you to use your time in a way that makes you happy. If you enjoy work and would rather work longer to live a lavish lifestyle, create a plan that will help you achieve those goals. If you want to build wealth while still enjoying life, you can make that happen too. Either way, our goal is that you don't wake up at age 60 and realize you didn't have a plan.

My plan didn't always include medicine. My dad actually told me ***not*** to go to medical school because it is a long, hard road and he didn't want me to work that hard for such little payout, because he knew I would go into pediatrics. So, as a rebellious college student, I decided to take the MCAT and apply to medical school instead of attending grad school to do biochemistry research. I went to medical school at the University of Kansas with in-state tuition and had help with living expenses from my parents. The only loans I took out were for tuition, yet my loans ballooned in residency and fellowship despite making monthly income-based repayments for public student loan forgiveness (PSLF).

While I was in medical school, Ryan was completing his master's in business administration (MBA) and master's in accounting and financial management, both from the University of San Diego. Ryan likes money—actually, he ***loves*** money. Aside from his family, nothing brings him more joy than growing something from nothing. He enjoys the journey more than the end result, and I think that's why he loves helping people with their financial plans. He wants physicians and their families to navigate their financial journeys with the highest probability of success. He's so invested in his mission he publishes three episodes a week about physician finance on the *Financial Residency* podcast.

Ryan has always warned me to be wary of people trying to sell products—insurance and investments—to residents and unsuspecting physicians. I was so wary of salespeople that I mistakenly thought my employer's 403(b) was a gimmick and did not enroll in the matching program. It was operated by an outside company and we had to enroll and select a payment deduction from our paychecks. It sounded sketchy and instead of asking Ryan, I assumed I knew what was going on. It wasn't until my third year of residency that I realized the mistake I had made. (I'm sorry, co-residents who listened to me and didn't sign up for a 403(b) during our intern year!) I had someone excellent and knowledgeable with finance living with me, and I didn't take five minutes to ask for his opinion. If I had contributed to a 403(b) with employer match for all three years of residency, I would have contributed an additional $33,500 pre-tax, and my employer would have matched 50% of that amount. Growing at 6% a year, if I retired at age 60, that money alone would have grown to over $250,000. That was a costly mistake for us. On the other end of the spectrum, some of our friends were sold whole life insurance policies during residency and didn't understand what they were purchasing. They paid thousands of dollars toward policies instead of paying down debt or investing.

During fellowship, Ryan and I made big financial decisions. We bought and sold our first home, we had two children, and we made big changes to our plan to reflect the future we wanted. I had many friends in the same boat who would ask Ryan for help. But what were physicians who didn't have access to Ryan and the podcast doing, and how were they making decisions? There is no "finance for poor residents" course, and most financial advisors are too costly for residents. Some of our friends had an "advisor" who told them to invest all of their extra money in the stock market rather than save for a house or pay off credit card debt. The reason they were given this advice was that the advisor was paid based on an assets under management (AUM) model, where the advisor only made money from their stock market investments.

Ryan saw a huge opportunity to help young physicians with significant debt plan for their financial futures, so he started Physician Wealth Services. As his business has grown, he has still dedicated his free time and much of his energy to helping physicians make good decisions to set themselves up for financial success through his podcast.

As a physician, it's up to you to seek out your own financial education because it isn't taught in school. You can hire a financial planner or learn to manage your finances on your own. Not everyone needs a financial planner. Many people are perfectly fine planning their own finances. But you might lack the knowledge you need to do it alone. If that's you, we wrote this book to help you take control of your financial future.

Taylor

Creating a financial plan follows the SOAP acronym concept, which you are familiar with: subjective, objective, assessment, and plan.

The subjective is soft data, whatever the patient says about their condition. In this case, you're the patient, and we need to gather the soft data on your financial life.

The objective is the hard facts, the data about the patient. From a financial standpoint, the objective component represents the basics of your finances: your bank accounts, income, assets, and the like. We will need to organize this black-and-white information in order to get to the assessment.

The assessment is the physician's view of what's going on based on the subjective and objective data. Financially, this is where you analyze what you have and come to a better understanding of your finances.

Finally, the plan is the next steps. Financially, this is where you take action to improve your financial life.

This book is packed with everything you need to know to make your own financial plan. Every chapter has some additional work you will complete as you go along. It's important to complete each exercise as you go because it will allow you to build your own financial plan in easy steps.

Along with the exercises in this book, you have access to a free course that includes the templates we use with our clients. There are short videos that explain how to use the templates so it's easy for you to fill them out. You'll collect these worksheets and at the end of the book, we will bring them all together so you can see your own financial plan, created by *you!* If you won't have internet access while reading this book, download all of the templates so you can use them as we go along.

This book is designed to be approachable and informative, written in, and referenced throughout the beginning part of your financial journey. You can feel good about sharing it with your friends, family, and colleagues, and we'd consider it an honor if you did. Start conversations with your colleagues about how they are reducing their financial stress by planning.

Go to FinancialFellowship.com and join our community of fellows taking control of their financial futures.

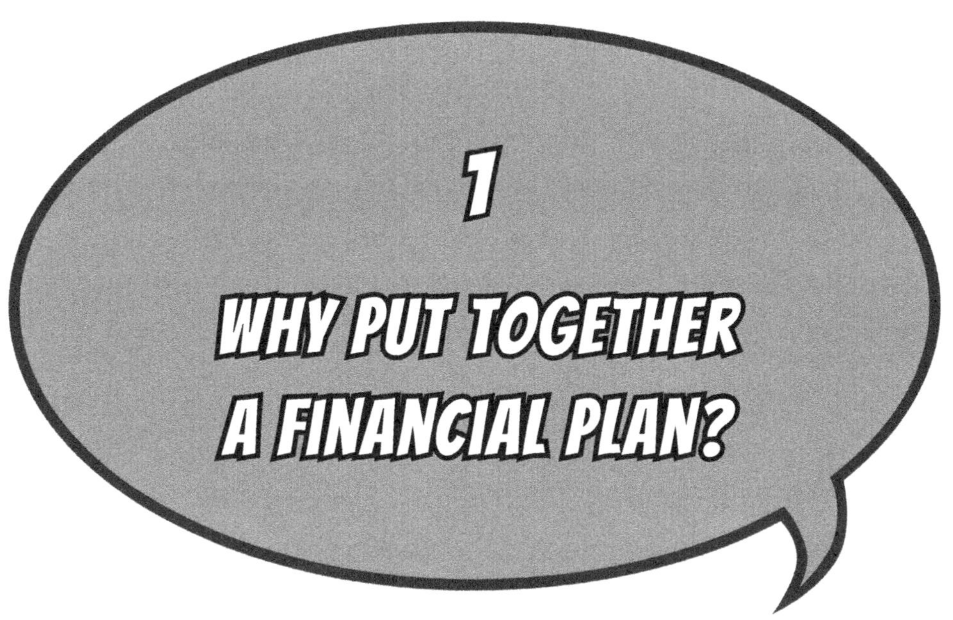

1
WHY PUT TOGETHER A FINANCIAL PLAN?

This write-as-you-go format will guide you through creating your own financial plan, but why should you put together a financial plan?

If you don't know what direction you're going with your finances, how do you know you're going in the ***right*** direction to achieve your goals?

Think about it like golf. If you just swung your club without looking at where the flag was or planning your shot, you would have no idea if you were hitting near the hole—the goal. It would be like playing golf at night—nearly impossible. Instead, you want to look at the flag, take note of any hazards in the way, like sand traps or trees, and plan your shot accordingly.

You approach your second shot the same way. If you started your financial journey without knowing where the flag was, you might have hit it behind a tree, making it harder to recover. Planning your next shots financially is critical to achieving your goal of getting the ball into the hole, whatever that looks like for you. Sometimes you will have to hit sideways to get out from behind the tree, and sometimes you will have to lay up because you can't hit it over that hazard.

The same holds true for financial planning and achieving your goals. Becoming a physician required you to go backward financially before you could go forward, taking on massive amounts of student debt and delaying your investment in retirement. While there are many benefits that come with being a doctor, there are many obstacles in your way.

The journey that physicians go through begins in high school, where you work hard to get good grades so you can get into a good college, and from college into med school, then from med school to a residency program, then potentially a fellowship, and finally to find a good job. During all of that, it's uncommon to stop and think, "Am I spending my money in a way that makes me happy? Am I allocating funds to live a more fulfilled life?"

When you're working 80 hours a week or more, it's just about survival. You're not focused on your financial future or your goals because you're too busy just getting through the work you have to do.

But now it's time to think about creating a financial plan that will help you achieve your goals. First, you have to identify what those goals are. What do you want out of life?

Use the SMART acronym to set better goals you're more likely to achieve. SMART stands for specific, measurable, achievable, realistic, and time bound. Maybe you write, "I want to get better with money." That isn't a SMART goal because it's not specific enough, there's no way for you to measure your success, and it isn't time bound. You need to put more parameters on it to hold yourself accountable.

To turn it into a SMART goal, you might write instead, "I want to save 10% of my take-home pay to build up an emergency fund in 2020. My target emergency fund is $20,000." This version of the goal is specific, measurable, achievable, realistic, and time bound.

What are your opportunities and goals in the next one, three, and five years?

One-year opportunities: ______________________________
____
____

One-year goals: ______________________________
____
____

Three-year opportunities: ______________________________
____
____

Three-year goals: ______________________________
____
____
____

Five-year opportunities: ______________________________
____
____

Five-year goals: ______________________________
____
____

What could possibly get in the way of achieving your goals?

1. ____
2. ____
3. ____

What are your concerns about the next one, three, and five years?

One year: ____

____

Three years: ____

____

Five years: ____

____

How will you address those concerns?

1. ____
2. ____
3. ____

What obstacles are in your way?

1. ____
2. ____
3. ____

Most physicians aren't thinking about these things. Your mindset around money needs to be right. You've pushed so hard for so long that it's easy to trap yourself by buying expensive things without stopping to think about what would truly make you happy.

The last thing you want is to suddenly wake up in your 50s and realize you don't have as many assets as you need to retire in the time frame you want. Don't let the lack of a plan stop you from realizing your optimal life.

I don't need to tell you how much burnout affects physicians. I see it so often with our clients. What I also see is how creating and implementing a financial plan can help shed light on how you want to live your life. It doesn't eliminate burnout, but it does improve your financial health, which will lead you to a happier, more prosperous life.

There are two attitudes physicians often have that get in the way of creating a financial plan and ultimately achieving their goals.

The first attitude is "I'm going to make so much money, why does it matter? I can just use cash flow and pay for anything I need or want." They think in monthly payments. "I can afford it because I can afford the monthly payment."

I had a conversation with a client who wanted to buy a Tesla. I asked, "Do you think you can afford a Tesla?"

"I make $30,000 a month, so yes."

"Great. Can you write a check for the Tesla?"

"No."

"Why do you think you can afford it if you can't write the $90,000 check?"

"Because I can afford the payment."

"If you can't afford the $90,000, what makes you think you're going to afford a car that will cost $110,000 with interest over five years? Can you afford $110,000?"

"No, I can't afford $90,000."

"Then you can't afford the car."

"Oh, I get what you're saying now. Buy it all in cash."

The second mindset physicians often have is "I'm so screwed. I have so much student debt, why am I budgeting? I've got a massive mortgage on my back and I'm a pediatrician." It seems hopeless, so they don't even try.

Either of these mindsets can keep you from achieving your goals, both financially and throughout your life. You must create a plan and stick to it in order to live the life you truly desire.

If you don't know the direction you're going, how do you know you're going in the right direction?

If you know what you want, put that first.

So why should you put together a plan? To become more intentional.

WHAT

Creating a financial plan is like making a road map for your life so you know where you're going and are more likely to achieve your goals.

WHY

A financial plan will keep you from going in the wrong direction or wandering aimlessly.

RESULT

Build a custom plan unique to your needs, your wishes, and your starting place to launch you on a better path to achieving your goals. This will create a foundation for you to build your ideal life.

In every chapter, you'll find resources you can write in or use to build your financial plan. If you'd like to have digital files of these resources, you can find them at **financialresidency.com/freecourse**. Some of the tools have been simplified to fit in the book, and the complimentary course will give you the full templates to fill in with more detail. These resources will be critical in your ability to build your own financial plan, so follow along and complete the exercises as you read.

2

DISCOVER YOUR IDEAL LIFE

To begin creating your financial plan, you need to understand your goals. What does your ideal life look like? The point of creating a financial plan is to help you achieve your ideal life—to live the lifestyle you want, to retire when you want, and to have enough money for the things that matter to you most. A financial plan will help you focus your spending and your savings on things that are important to you, not just things you ***should*** be spending on and saving for.

The first step is to identify your goals. Keep these in mind with every step of your financial plan.

What are your top five goals in life?

1. ______________________________
2. ______________________________
3. ______________________________
4. ______________________________
5. ______________________________

Write them out in a list. They don't have to be financial goals—write whatever your top goals are for your life. Don't worry if this isn't easy to start with. We'll go over some exercises to help you think through them.

If you're married, your spouse should write their goals out separately. Then you'll compare, and you might be surprised by what you find. You need to complete these exercises together so you know what's important to each other and can work together to accomplish those things. You both need to be involved with your finances because if one person has no say, their goals will never be realized. This must be a joint effort.

Below are two simple exercises—the airport test and the one-year letter—you can use as a way to cement these ideas in your mind. It's okay if these exercises feel somewhat repetitive. There will be differences in your answers each time you complete an exercise. Give yourself time to work through them and really think about your desires and goals.

EXERCISE 1 (THE AIRPORT TEST)

Imagine you run into a friend at the airport in the future, and you haven't seen them for five or more years. They ask you, "What have you been doing the past five years? I haven't seen you!"

What would you tell that person if you were living your ideal life? What could you tell them that would truly make you fulfilled and happy if it were true?

Through this exercise, you've begun to think about how you view success. Let's go into more detail now and put together a success timeline.

Think about the next one, five, 10, and 30 years. What would need to occur in each given time frame for you to feel happy and successful? Dream big and write it all down. What would allow you to truly feel fulfilled and happy in the life that you have chosen to live?

This isn't just financial. Think of all aspects of your life and how you want to live a healthy and fulfilled life.

Here is an example to get you started.

1 Year	5 Years	10 Years	30 Years
Pay down some debt.	Become a partner in my practice.	Shop without having to worry about prices.	I'm financially independent.
Continue to build my career and learn.	I'm married with a healthy kid (maybe two).	Only have mortgage debt.	I have a healthy and active lifestyle.
Move into a new-to-us home.	PSLF works, and student debt is gone!	College funds are in place and I make regular contributions.	I've raised intelligent and respectful kids.
	Emergency fund is in place.		

What does your ideal success timeline look like?

1 Year	5 Years	10 Years	30 Years

EXERCISE 2 (THE ONE-YEAR LETTER)

Write a letter to yourself now that you will read one year from now. The letter should encourage you to take action on things you want to accomplish within the next year. Tell your future self that you better have accomplished those things.

When you read the letter in a year, it'll give you time to pause and think about how the last year went. Did you accomplish what you wanted? If not, what were the obstacles? If you did, what were the good things that came out of it?

It's easy to forget about your goals and what you have accomplished so far. The letter acts as a type of plan and also allows you to reflect and see how much you actually have accomplished.

In addition to outlining your goals, you should identify your opportunities and your challenges. Within the next three years, what are the good things coming up? What are the big obstacles in your way? Opportunities might include a new job, starting a family or adding to it, and traveling more. The obstacles are what could get in the way of those things, such as student loans and housing expenses.

Take the opportunities and challenges you wrote about in chapter 1 and make changes if necessary after you've identified your biggest goals. These will inform your planning as you go through this book. It's best to address obstacles and opportunities head-on at the beginning of the financial planning process rather than deal with them later, when it will be more difficult to make changes.

It's never too early to start thinking about your goals and your ideal life. Where do you picture yourself in five years? Ten years? Our life goals have shifted over the years but as we have gotten older the shifts have not been as drastic. Our big goal of raising our children together and keeping our family our number one priority has stayed the same. When big decisions come up (like moving to a new city for a job), it's easier to discuss the pros and cons knowing what our long-term goals are. We have had some major moves over the years and finally feel settled. If we did not have our long-term goals in mind, it would have been easy to overspend on a house and not have money left over for traveling, which is important to us.

WHAT'S YOUR IDEAL SCHEDULE BY DAY, MONTH, AND YEAR?

When thinking about your ideal life, it's easiest to frame it in terms of what your ideal schedule would look like. What would an ideal day look like? How about an ideal year? If you didn't have to worry about money or work or anything, what would you want your life to look like?

What would your ideal day look like?

What would your ideal month look like?

What would your ideal year look like?

____

____

____

____

____

____

____

____

____

____

Again, complete this exercise with your spouse if you're married. Each person answers for their own day, month, and year. Then compare and contrast. Usually there's something that will surprise you about your spouse's answer—maybe you didn't know how important something was to them.

The point of this exercise is to help you visualize what your ideal life would be so you can work toward achieving it.

To help you identify what's most important to you, George Kinder has developed three questions. Answer the questions one at a time and don't skip ahead. These questions give you perspective on how your life and money intersect so you can begin to shape your finances around what matters most to you.

George Kinder's three questions* should be answered in the following order:

1. I want you to imagine that you are financially secure, that you have enough money to take care of your needs, now and in the future. How would you live your life? Would you change anything? Let yourself go. Don't hold back on your dreams. Describe a life that is complete, that is richly yours.

2. This time you visit your doctor who tells you that you have only 5-10 years left to live. The good part is that you won't ever feel sick. The bad news is that you will have no notice of the moment of your death. What will you do in the time you have remaining to live? Will you change your life, and how will you do it?

3. This time your doctor shocks you with the news that you have only one day left to live. Notice what feelings arise as you confront your very real mortality. Ask yourself, what did I miss? Who did I not get to be? What did I not get to do?

*This material was developed by George Kinder and the Kinder Institute of Life Planning. It is part of a program of trainings that lead to the Registered Life Planner® designation. Used by permission of George Kinder © 1999, 2009, 2019.

I took time off after fellowship to be a mom and spend time with our two kids, who were both under age 2. We moved somewhere with a lower cost of living so I would have invaluable time with our babies. When it was time for me to start looking for a long-term job, I wrote out a job description for my ideal job. It included things like "walking kids to school once a week" and "work-life balance" and even "being home by 4:30 p.m. on most days." I didn't share these "slacker" goals while interviewing, but I was better able to assess if a job would be a good fit because I had my goals in mind. At one job interview, one of the interviewers asked what my goals were and my first reply was "Work-life balance." I ended up not even getting a courtesy call after my interview. I was disappointed at first, but I later learned that practice would have been a horrible long-term choice for a career. I spoke about the same goal when interviewing for my current job and it was much more accepted, which gave me the reassurance that I would be supported. I could not be happier where I am now—I work hard but I can set my hours and walk the kids to school once a week.

Taylor

WHAT

Life planning is the process of discovering what's truly important to you beyond just your financial data.

WHY

Establish what's important to you so you can build your finances around your goals. There's more to finance than numbers. Build your financial life in a way that makes you happy.

RESULT

This will allow you to identify the important things that need to be included and prioritized within your life and finances in order for you to feel fulfilled.

COURSE

It's helpful to use exercises and questions to discover what's most important to you. My favorites are George Kinder's three questions to determine your ideal life, which I use with all of my clients. Complete them one at a time and don't move on to the next before you've completed the first. If you prefer to type your responses, you can find the questions by going to the complimentary course at **financialresidency.com/freecourse**.

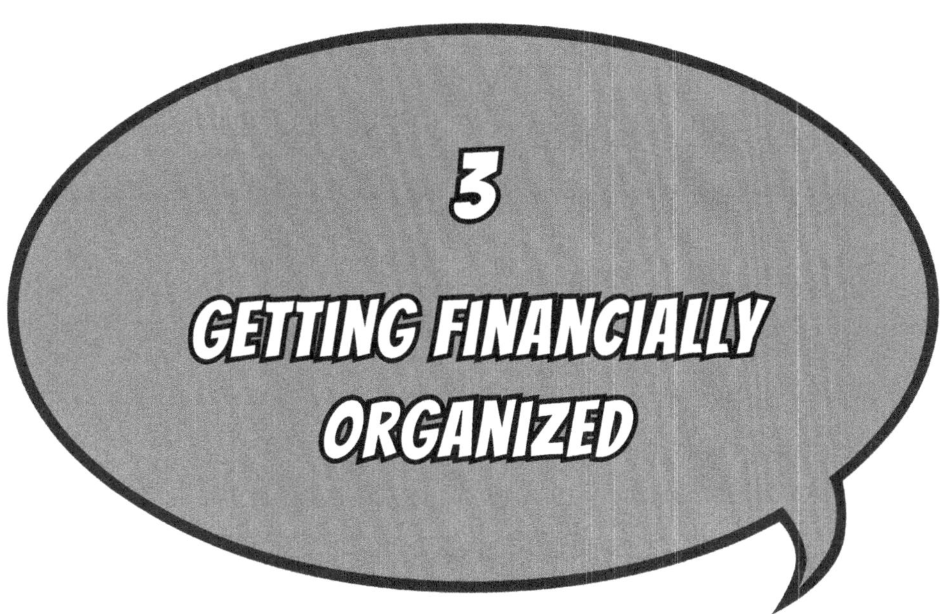

3

GETTING FINANCIALLY ORGANIZED

Getting financially organized is similar to living a healthy lifestyle. We all know what it takes to stay healthy—eating right, exercising regularly, and avoiding stress—yet it's an entirely different challenge to actually do those things.

The same is true for organizing your financial life. You may know what you should be doing, but it's challenging to put into action.

One of the top reasons it's hard to get started organizing your finances is that it seems so overwhelming. You need to monitor multiple accounts, download apps, and check statements—and don't forget all the documents that need filing.

Getting financially organized is similar to ordering labs for a patient. You have to understand what's happening with your finances—the good, the bad, and the ugly—before you can diagnose problems and then prescribe a plan to improve your finances. In this step, you will take note of your financial data and start the organization of your financial documents.

Organizing your financial data can seem overwhelming when you first begin because there's so much to keep track of. As a physician, it can be hard to find the time to stay on top of everything and make sure your bills get paid on time, let alone keep all your files in order. Slow down and take a deep breath. The best way to approach anything is one step at a time.

So how do we begin tracking your financial data? It starts by creating a financial mind map. In this exercise, you will take inventory of your finances. This is a high-level scan where you note basic things like how many credit cards you have, where your bank accounts are located, the number of loans you have and their amounts, and your assets.

Getting your finances organized does not mean you must have everything perfectly neat before you move on. Right now, it's just dumping everything onto paper. Use the mind map template below to start organizing your thoughts into the appropriate sections.

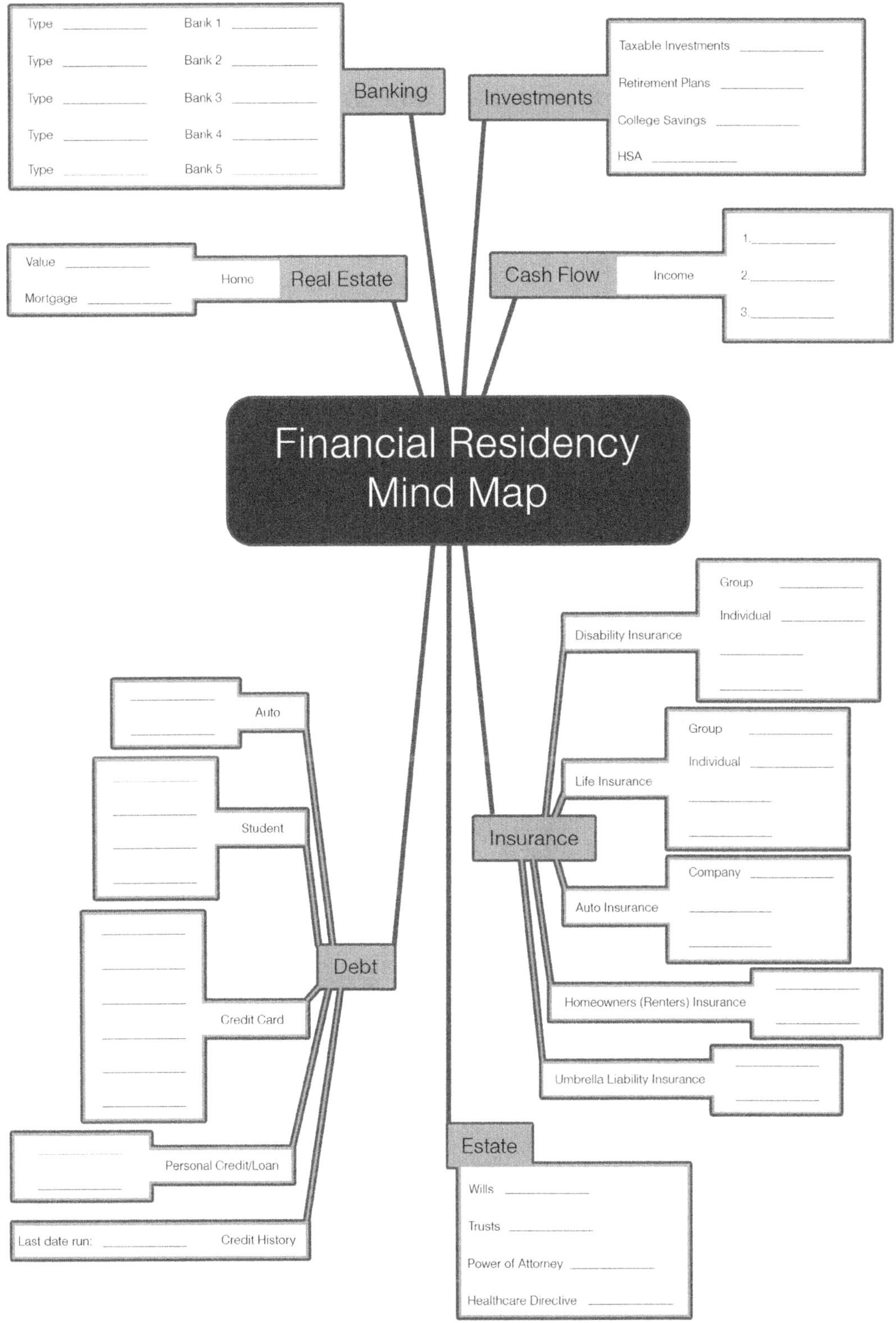
Financial Residency Mind Map
Banking
Type
Type
Type
Type
Type
Bank 1
Bank 2
Bank 3
Bank 4
Bank 5
Investments
Taxable Investments
Retirement Plans
College Savings
HSA
Real Estate
Home
Value
Mortgage
Cash Flow
Income
1.
2.
3.
Insurance
Disability Insurance
Group
Individual
Life Insurance
Group
Individual
Auto Insurance
Company
Homeowners (Renters) Insurance
Umbrella Liability Insurance
Debt
Auto
Student
Credit Card
Personal Credit/Loan
Credit History
Last date run:
Estate
Wills
Trusts
Power of Attorney
Healthcare Directive

Below is an overview of documents you should include in your organization system so you always know where they are:

Banking

- ❑ Copy of most recent bank statement

Cash Flow

- ❑ Most recent pay stubs for all employment
- ❑ Other income sources (e.g., rental property statements)

Debt

- ❑ Credit report (do a quick review to make sure data is correct)
- ❑ Student debt statement (include latest confirmation of PSLF-qualified months)
- ❑ Car loan statement
- ❑ Mortgage statement
- ❑ Credit card statement (only if balance is carried)
- ❑ Personal loan statement

Insurance Declaration/Summary Pages

- ❑ Auto
- ❑ Home (or renter)
- ❑ Disability
- ❑ Business
- ❑ Professional liability
- ❑ Health
- ❑ Life
- ❑ Umbrella
- ❑ Annuities
- ❑ Any life insurance policies on which you are a beneficiary

Employee Benefits/Business

- ❑ Employee benefits packet (needs to include info on group insurance, retirement benefits, and healthcare plan chosen)
- ❑ Contract with employer/partnership
- ❑ LLC/S-corporation organization agreement

Investments

- ❑ Most recent statement for all investment accounts
- ❑ 401(k), 403(b), IRA, HSA, taxable, and any other retirement savings accounts
- ❑ Screenshot of the investment selections held in your employer retirement investment accounts
- ❑ Any other assets (business interests, real estate, etc.)

Taxes

- ❑ Past two years of tax returns (federal, state, corporate, or other returns)
- ❑ Receipts for tax-deductible expenses over current year

Estate

- ❑ Copies of all executed estate documents (will(s), power of attorney form(s), and trust(s))

Personal

- ❑ Social Security cards, birth certificates, and other forms of ID
- ❑ Marriage or divorce certificates

With this information, you'll create a folder system and use it to improve your financial structure, but it's important to simply understand what you have first. It will benefit you to know where everything relating to your finances is located and to have it all written in one place so you don't forget important details.

The point of this exercise is so you understand where you are with your finances and whether it's good or bad, with no judgment. This will make organizing easier in the future. For now, just take inventory. Don't feel guilty—just be objective with the facts about what exists.

Once you've written everything down, you will find additional ways to improve your organization throughout this book.

While completing the financial mind map, take the time to ensure you understand your debt. How much money do you owe, and to whom?

Facing debt head-on can be one of the most overwhelming steps in understanding your larger financial picture, especially for physicians, who average hundreds of thousands of dollars in student loan debt. But to get organized, you have to know exactly what you owe.

To establish a strategy to pay down debt, you have to look at it line by line. Whether you think you know the exact amounts or you've been afraid to look at your statements in detail, take time to get the exact numbers on paper.

After completing the mind map, dedicate some time to cleaning up places where documents tend to accumulate.

ORGANIZE YOUR SNAIL MAIL

Believe it or not, getting financially organized begins at the mailbox. Even in today's digital world, we still have to deal with mail. Most of it is probably junk, but occasionally you receive something that needs your attention.

Let's review a familiar scenario. You come home, check the mail, and throw the stack of envelopes and junk mail on the counter. You make an empty promise to look through it later and make sure there's nothing important. The mail continues to sit, waiting patiently for your review, yet you never look at it. It just sits until you need to dig through it to find one item. You spend more time trying to find the important paper you need. You get the point.

If you want to get your finances organized, you need to start with the paper entering your home. No matter how exhausted you are from your long shift, it will only take a moment to purge. Grab your mail every day and quickly decide what should stay or go. Chances are most of the paper in the stack can go straight into the recycling bin.

Now that you have the junk out of the way, you can see if any mail needs a follow-up. The important items need to be filed somewhere easy to find them later on.

Ryan and I have a system where I check the mail each day and purge the junk mail right away. (How many pizza coupons does one family need?) Next, I take the mail that needs a follow-up and put it in Ryan's office. We have two inboxes: one for urgent mail and one where a response is needed within the month. From there, Ryan can easily review and we know exactly where everything is located. Luckily, we don't receive too many urgent items through snail mail, so it doesn't take long to file what needs to be reviewed.

Once we've responded to the mail, it gets filed in the appropriate place.

It may sound basic, but it keeps important items from slipping through the cracks. It forces us to be more organized. Otherwise, the mail would collect dust on the dining room table.

Taylor

ORGANIZE YOUR INBOX

If paper is a cause of clutter in your life, then email is probably even more of a nightmare. Communication via email has become the normal way of life, and just like the pesky junk mail that sits in your mailbox, spam emails pile up in your inbox.

An easy way to achieve a more organized financial life is to get your email inbox under control. Do you have thousands of unread emails, so the number has become almost like a badge of honor?

Most likely your massive inbox causes you to waste time searching for important information. Even worse, you feel anxious when you open up your email because you have no idea what needs a response and what's junk.

There are lots of tricks to organizing your email, but let me tell you about the system I personally use. My personal email is organized into four categories: needs response, needs review, awaiting response, and everything else.

The categories are pretty self-explanatory. I find this system super helpful to keep me on track. Once I respond to something from the "needs response" category, I archive it. If I am awaiting a response from someone I sent an email to, I label the email "awaiting response." For less urgent emails, I mark "needs review," and when it's convenient for me, I spend some time working through those emails with the goal of reaching zero emails in my inbox.

That's it—nothing magical or complicated. But it definitely keeps me from getting behind or missing important emails.

Without a system to organize email, it becomes overwhelming and chaotic. You wouldn't go up to your mailbox and take out one piece of mail and then leave the rest in the mailbox. But we constantly do that for our emails. It doesn't make sense, but it's something we all do. Get in the habit of batching emails together and organizing them based on whether you need to review or respond. I'd even encourage you to take it a step further and unsubscribe from the promotional emails you never read. These emails tempt you to purchase things you probably don't need, and unsubscribing to them will create fewer emails for you to go through.

ORGANIZE YOUR DOCUMENTS

Once you've responded to your emails and paper bills, it's time to file the important items away. You may wonder what the best filing system is for your home office.

The best filing system is the one you remember to use and that makes it easy for you to locate items.

Generally, it's best to keep separate folders for all of your financial papers. Within the financial files, organize your records related to taxes, your personal and retirement accounts, and insurance policies.

You should have a separate folder for any legal documents you need to keep records for. This includes information related to your estate planning, passports, birth certificates, and all other important legal items.

Don't forget to file all information related to your student loan debt, especially if you are seeking public service loan forgiveness, because you will need records to qualify.

Once you have everything in place, create a backup system. You could take pictures or scan the documents into a cloud storage system. You never know when you could lose the physical copies of your files, so do yourself a favor and create an easy backup.

Lastly, create a naming convention for your files that is easy for you to remember and other people to access if necessary. Come up with labels so someone else could find the info in case they needed to.

I hope you now see there are very easy tasks you can start today to get your financial life organized. Think about the amount of time you waste when you don't know where things are. Then think about how much money you waste each year when you pay your bills too late and rack up late fees.

Yes, it does seem like there are a lot of things to organize for your finances. Unfortunately, there's not a way to make all these tasks go away. What you can do, however, is go step by step to achieve an organized financial life.

Remember, an organized financial life saves you time and money.

My younger brother was in a motorcycle accident during my pulmonary fellowship. We were overwhelmed dealing with his immediate medical care, but we also needed to file claims with auto insurance and handle other paperwork. I was so impressed to find a small, portable file organizer where my younger brother, a "fly by the seat of his pants" type, had everything neatly organized. It made dealing with paperwork so much easier for us. Typically I don't like to prep for doomsday, but this was super helpful. My brother is doing great now. (And I'm hoping he's still just as organized!)

Taylor

DIGESTIBLE TIPS

WHAT

Getting financially organized begins with a brain dump: taking everything in your head, putting it on paper, and then sorting all the data into organized formats.

WHY

This process equates to taking labs for a patient. You want to understand what you're dealing with before you can diagnose and prescribe. You need the financial data before you can begin to make changes.

RESULT

You'll be left with a one-page snapshot of everything going on in your financial life and a file system that actually works.

COURSE

Getting financially organized is much easier with the templates we use with our clients. In this chapter, you began to organize your data with the mind map template and the financial checklist. You'll find digital versions of these templates and a video about how to use them at **financialresidency.com/freecourse**.

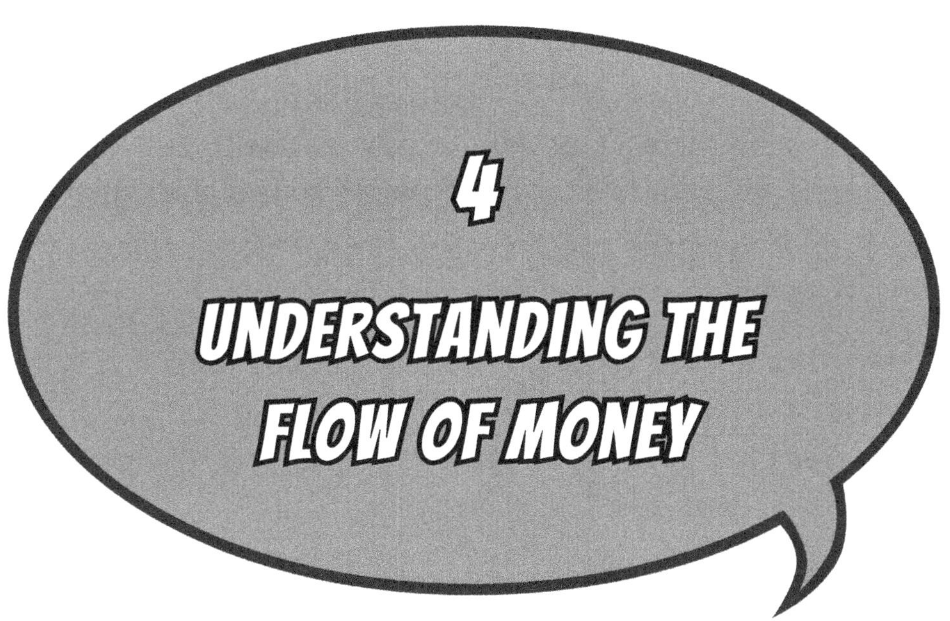

4

UNDERSTANDING THE FLOW OF MONEY

If the idea of a budget gives you anxiety or stress, you're not alone. For many, the word "budget" feels restricting, like it takes all the fun out of the life you have worked so hard to build. Or it might feel like just one more thing to keep up with while your schedule is hectic. I get it.

I call budgeting "the dreaded B-word," but the reason it gets a bad reputation is because budgeting is a target. It's something you are "aiming" for. Implementing the right type of budget is crucial because if you don't have a target, you'll just be shooting blind.

I'm not here to talk about a budget that is flat and one-dimensional. There's not a single correct way to make a budget. It should have room for your personality. It should take into account your vision for your future so your goals and dreams will be realized.

Most physicians look at a budget as a constraint, but it's actually what sets you free.

If we look at traditional budgeting, it's about looking ***back*** at your finances—what you've spent in the past and what your financial habits are. This tends to bring up negative emotions about what you didn't do right or areas where you overspent and usually ends with you just quitting.

Looking forward and creating a plan for how you will spend in the future is cash flow planning or what I call a "living budget." That's where I want you to be—looking toward the future and planning your cash flow needs so you can achieve your goals.

A lot of physicians don't understand why tracking your spending is important, which makes sense. Learning how to build the correct budget doesn't just happen, especially for people who have never been exposed to successful financial planning. I strongly believe that everyone needs to do cash flow planning, but unless you know how much you spend in detail, you will need to look back before you can move forward.

Physicians typically have enough income each month to cover their expenses with room to spare, so they think a budget shouldn't be high on their priority list. This could work out fine for you, especially if you are saving and investing that money automatically. However, that is unlikely to be the case, and creating a budget and sticking to it shows you where your money is going each month. This will allow you to save and invest even more so you can build more wealth in the future.

I want to help you build a budget that doesn't make you feel like you are in prison. Let's craft your own living budget.

To set a baseline where you will start tracking your spending, fill in the lines next to each category with what you think you are spending in that particular category. Take your best guess and don't be afraid to be wrong. Just know that based on the hundreds of times we have done this with clients, your guess will be off—sometimes really far off—and that's totally fine. We have to start somewhere!

Auto/Transportation ______________________

Bills/Utility ______________________

Debt ______________________

Food ______________________

Health ______________________

Home ______________________

Insurance ______________________

Family ______________________

Lifestyle Spending ______________________

Travel ______________________

Amazon ______________________

Here are the percentages we recommend spending in each category:

- Auto/Transportation: 4%
- Bills/Utility: 6%
- Debt: 31%

- Food: 10%
- Health: 2%
- Home: 9%
- Insurance: 5%
- Family: 8%
- Lifestyle Spending: 16%
- Travel: 5%
- Amazon: 4%

Now, everyone's finances are different, but if you want to model your finances after our family's, what you just filled in are the categories we use in our day-to-day living budget. Yes, for our family, Amazon actually has its own category. I'm sure they get a chunk of your paycheck too, and if that's the case, you should track it.

You might notice there isn't a miscellaneous category. That is because a miscellaneous category can quickly become a black hole and should be avoided. Anything you might consider miscellaneous should go into the lifestyle category.

Now it's time to begin creating your living budget. There are six major steps in creating a living budget:

1. Determine your goals.
2. Review your finances.
3. Rank spending.
4. Apply the formula.
5. Track spending.
6. Set up the correct banking structure.

We'll cover each of these in detail in this chapter.

DETERMINE YOUR FINANCIAL GOALS

Before we get started with the analysis of your spending, we need to get on the same page about what you want to accomplish. This will allow you to associate positive emotions with your finances and help keep you on track when the going gets tough. Write down some of your short-term and long-term financial goals.

An example of a short-term goal (occurring within six months to two years) could be creating an emergency fund. Long-term goals are for what you would like to accomplish two to five years down the road, like buying a home.

In addition to your goals, you need to pinpoint your priorities in spending. Priorities could be things such as comfortable housing, keeping the car operating, or quality childcare. Your priorities could go beyond the scope of money and could include spending on things such as date nights, birthday and holiday celebrations, and paying down debt.

What are you saving for?

What is the money going to be used for?

Use these questions to help you determine your goals and priorities as you write them in the spaces on the next page.

Short-Term Goals (six months to two years)

Long-Term Goals (two or more years)

Priorities in Your Spending

*For more space, you can download our templates in the free companion course at financialresidency.com/freecourse.

If you are married, include your spouse in this planning. Usually, with married couples, one person seems to know all the details about where the money is going and the other person is completely oblivious. This isn't healthy, and this is where regular "money talks" are ideal. You can even make it a "money date." (I joke and say it's getting "financially frisky" with your spouse; I know, I'm a nerd.)

These money dates don't have to be boring and stressful. By all means, make them as enjoyable as possible by doing things that you both find fun. Maybe send the kids away to a babysitter, put on some music, and prepare or order a nice meal while talking numbers.

During your money date, discuss upcoming bills, extra expenses such as school clothes or school supplies, and decide who is going to take care of handling each task, bill, or expense. It's also good to discuss your goals as a family, such as vacations, travel, or family outings that you'd like to take.

Spend your money where it excites you.

I struggle with the budgeting concept. I want to go shopping when it's convenient for me without planning ahead and putting it in a spreadsheet. I'm not sure what Ryan does to make this work—maybe he should share his secrets here! When we first got married we merged our bank accounts but also had separate accounts so we both had spending money without feeling guilty. Frankly, I was bad at handling separate bank accounts. I had a separate credit card but I would always forget to use it for spending money. Eventually we merged everything together. Merging our accounts increased transparency and allowed us to have better conversations about our finances. We stopped thinking in terms of "mine and yours" and instead thought in terms of "ours." Our separate accounts were like training wheels for married finances—like learning to ride a normal bike, we outgrew the need.

Taylor

REVIEW YOUR FINANCES

During the first month or two of budgeting, just observe where your money is going. Don't try to change your budget yet, because you don't know where the money is being spent. You can't prescribe changes without diagnosing what is going on.

I don't want you to go on a strict diet (budget), because too much restriction can cause you to rebound. You don't need that type of negativity in your financial life. Slow and steady will create the most profound changes in your finances.

Reviewing your spending not only gives you a moment to check your own habits, but it also gives you time to make sure everyone else is billing you appropriately. You may find subscriptions you forgot to cancel or incorrect charges by people or services that bill you automatically.

RANK SPENDING

As you go through the review process, I encourage you to rank the categories in which you spend by what brings you the most happiness. You can only assign a dollar to one task, so why not spend it where it can bring the most happiness?

Rank the spending categories you chose in terms of necessity and happiness. For instance, paying your student loans is number one on the list for necessity but not necessarily for happiness. It will likely be helpful to break down the categories into subcategories so you can get an accurate picture of your rankings.

The power of putting a living budget in place and using it regularly relies on spending intentionally. You have to figure out what makes you happy and then budget and plan around that. Make your money work for you in the way that makes you the happiest.

For some people, an extravagant house may be what makes them happy. For others, it may be a smaller house but a beautiful, brand-new truck. Some people may not care about big fancy houses or cars at all. Maybe it's expensive vacations to exotic places, eating at extravagant restaurants, or traveling the globe and going on great adventures.

After tracking your spending for a few months, you will see a clear pattern of where your money is going. It doesn't matter what it is; just make sure that what you're spending your money on lines up with what makes you happy.

APPLY THE FORMULA

After you have reviewed your expenditures and ranked them by importance, it's time to set some bumpers or guidelines on how much you should be spending. I have a simple formula I encourage physicians to use for budgeting:

- 50% of your take-home pay goes toward fixed expenses (after taxes, 401(k), and other deductions).
- 25% of your take-home pay goes toward variable expenses (travel, concerts, lunches, and Starbucks).
- 25% of your take-home goes toward savings (anything that increases your net worth). This means saving for future travel or your kid's 529 plan does not count as part of these savings. Those do not increase your net worth because they are future expenses and should be included in variable expenses. While you may not be at a 25% savings rate, it's the target we want you to try to achieve.

TRACK SPENDING

Part of budgeting is learning to assess your trajectory. Are you on target? Are the results good, bad, or neutral? Is there a problem? If there is a problem, how do you fix it?

After applying the formula and understanding where your money is going, start planning ahead and estimating what you ***will spend*** rather than looking back at what you spent. Each month, take a small amount of time to review the past month and assess if you had the correct targets and address any issues that arose during the month.

As you go through this exercise, make a note of things you want to adjust. Chances are you'll have some things you want to change after you review a few months' worth of spending. You might even take this time to call your cell phone company, cable company, and other subscription services to ask for a reduced rate.

Remember, if you spend more than budgeted in a category, it's not the end of the world. You simply need to adjust again. Ultimately, practice makes perfect, and having a budget gives you a deeper understanding of your finances, which can enable you to build more wealth in the future.

SET UP THE CORRECT BANKING STRUCTURE

Out of all the tips I give you, this may be the one that changes your life. To successfully implement the living budget, you must set up the correct banking structure so you can automate your finances and control your flow of money. By creating an infrastructure that matches your plans for your money, you can easily see your spendable dollars and non-spendable dollars. The banking structure should take away the temptation to spend non-spendable money.

Taylor and I have one personal checking account at *one* bank. If you have multiple banks, cut it back to one. I can understand if the mortgage company requires you to have an account with them, but aside from those requirements, all your banking should be completed at one bank. Keep it simple!

With a single checking account, all of our money flows into this account. Our fixed expenses and bills are paid out of this account on an automated schedule. This takes a load off my mind. I won't forget due dates, and I don't have to waste time every month paying bills. I think the most important side effect is I get to spend time with my wife and children—time that we all value.

We set up an auto-transfer to move a portion of the money that comes into the main checking account into separate savings accounts marked for specific purposes. They're designated and titled for the goals we outlined.

For example, because our dog gets sick or hurt all the time, we have a savings account titled "Bear"—my dog's name. We contribute $50 a month to that account because he's going to get bit by a rattlesnake or something, and I'll have to take him to the vet. We also have a travel fund. Your savings accounts will be different than ours, depending on the needs of your family and on your savings goals.

Put emotion into your finances to help you stay on track with your savings. Say you're planning a trip to Australia. Create a special savings account for that and title it, "Family trip to Australia." Are you likely to take funds from your family trip to Australia to spend on something else? Probably not.

What does our bank structure look like? See below.

Main Checking

Emergency Savings

Sinking Fund

Family Trip to Australia

Bear

Home Projects

Tax

As you can see, we have an emergency savings account that we don't touch—and you shouldn't touch yours either. You want to be prepared for those events, right? Keep it separate from everything else.

Whatever unforeseen issue occurs in your life, it's never at a convenient time. Being financially prepared for an emergency is one of the best strategies. You should aim for three to six months of emergency funds, but this is a goal and don't worry if you can't do that right now. Start small by putting aside one month of total expenses and work up from there.

SINKING FUNDS

You probably noticed a savings account named "sinking fund." Everyone has expenses that are monthly, but we also have expenses that are quarterly, semiannual, or annual. Think of car insurance—you know it's coming. You know the amount. Why are you surprised when you have to pay it? You should be saving that same amount every month into a sinking fund and then when you pay that bill, transfer that amount from your savings to your checking.

Christmas comes at the same time every year, and birthdays come at the same time every year. Why is everyone so surprised when their budget gets blown in December? Save for it all year long. If you spend $600 on Christmas gifts, put $50 a month into a fund for that. No one should be surprised.

Sinking funds are a great way to slowly save up for the expenses you know you will have each year that are hard to plan for. A sinking fund will help you get ahead of an expense instead of being caught off guard.

At this point in the process, it's important to understand where your money is going, but don't begin making changes yet. You have to make changes systematically to make a difference and be sustainable. At the end of the book, we will put together everything we've done and create a cash flow plan that works with your budget.

Your goal right now is to know what all of your expenses are and how much you pay every month, plus your sinking expenses.

Remember, make your money work for you.

DIGESTIBLE TIPS

WHAT

Analyze how you're spending money and develop a spending plan free of guilt.

WHY

Align your spending with what makes you happiest and ensure you prioritize your goals.

RESULT

Understand how your money comes in and goes out so you can adjust your spending.

I hope the resources in this chapter will allow you to see an example of where your money could go as it comes into and leaves your bank account. In the free course, you'll see a copy of my personal budget. I've also created an example of my banking structure and a flowchart to show you the correct flow of money. These resources can be found at **financialresidency.com/freecourse**.

5

UNDERSTANDING AND CONFRONTING YOUR DEBT

A lot of people think all debt is bad debt. But that's not the case. There's good debt and bad debt. Some debt is necessary, like student debt. However, in order to be financially independent, you shouldn't have debt. To retire, you *shouldn't* have a mortgage. So you need to look at debt strategically—when you take it on and how you pay it off—to set yourself up for success.

Student debt is good debt, because essentially you're buying a business. If you think about the pricing of student debt like a business, it makes a lot of sense. Say you're going to make $300,000 a year as a doctor and had to take on $300,000 of debt to be able to do that. That's one times earnings. No business sells for that good of a deal. You can't buy any business for one times earnings—even a service business.

Now if you took on $800,000 in student loans to become a pediatrician and you make $200,000 a year, that was a bad decision. But for most physicians, student debt is not a bad thing. You just have to approach paying it off like paying business debt.

Let's talk about the different forms of debt you might have and how to deal with them.

STUDENT DEBT

When you're dealing with student debt, the big decision is whether you're going for public service loan forgiveness (PSLF) or not.

If you are, you need to have the right type of employer (they must be a 501(c)(3)), have only direct loans, and be on an income-driven repayment plan for 120 payments. Those are the requirements if you want to receive public service loan forgiveness. If you fail to meet any of those requirements, you will not be eligible to participate in that program.

It's important to remember you are required to make 120 payments, and you should get those payments approved (using the employment certification form) every 12 months. You'll need to keep track of all your payments because the servicers track things poorly. After 120 payments, your loans are forgiven. That means your payments in residency matter—even those $0 payments count toward your total of 120, meaning that you will have to pay less in the long run if you begin making those $0 payments while you're in residency. A common misconception is that the 120 payments need to be consecutive, but that is false. You just need to have 120 total approved payments meeting all the other criteria.

How do you determine whether PSLF is right for you? A general rule is if your debt is two times your expected salary or more, you should go for the forgiveness option. For example, if you're going to make $175,000 a year and your debt's more than $350,000, you should definitely consider going for public service loan forgiveness, because it will allow you to get rid of your debt faster than if you were to pay it off on your own.

Let's imagine you have $500,000 of debt and you only make $175,000 a year, but your current job allows you to obtain PSLF. You are offered a new position at a new employer for $225,000, but it would be in private practice, meaning that you will not qualify for PSLF. While the increase of $50,000 a year in salary seems nice, there are some potentially massive problems with taking this position. Due to not being able to lower your interest rate on your federal loans, mathematically, it would likely result in needing to refinance your loans. However, almost your whole paycheck would still go to your student debt. You can't afford that payment! You would also give up the opportunity to go for PSLF, which would likely have resulted in hundreds of thousands of dollars being forgiven, tax-free, by the government. Even making $50,000 more a year (before tax), it's ***very*** unlikely that you would make more money after tax, for all the years you worked there combined, than the amount that would be forgiven. Short-term gratification (making more money now) would cost you hundreds of thousands in the long run. Ouch.

If you're 100% sure you're not going for PSLF, then while you're in residency, you should still be on an income-driven repayment plan. I've created a free resource to help you better understand your repayment options. **Go to financialresidency.com/loanbuddy.** It's a calculator where you input information about your income, your family, and your lifestyle, and it will tell you the best loan repayment option for you. This is a free and easy way to understand your loan repayment options.

If you're an attending and you aren't going for PSLF, you will likely want to refinance your loans. The goal should be to pay off your loans in five to seven years, so pick a repayment option that will help you achieve this.

During residency and fellowship, I was enrolled in PSLF and made the minimum monthly payments toward my student loans. Over those six years (five years in the program before refinancing), my student loans ballooned to 140% of where I started. We were not sure what our long-term plans would be, so we set aside extra money that would have gone toward student loans and invested it ourselves. When we made the decision for me to take time off after fellowship, we made paying off my student loans a priority and refinanced at a lower interest rate.

Taylor

AUTO AND CONSUMER DEBT

Sometimes consumer debt and auto debt are necessary. You might have had to take on credit card debt to survive training. Getting into credit card debt to pay for your interviews is understandable. Try to minimize it, but it might be a necessity. Overspending on entertainment or dining out isn't worth it, and if this is the cause of your credit card debt, quit that kind of spending now. Work on your relationship with money before the stakes are higher. Your future self will thank you.

If you are in consumer debt while you're in training because you are the primary breadwinner and you have kids, it's okay. Try to limit it to $20,000 maximum. Any more than that will cause a real strain on your cash flow when you become an attending.

Auto debt is also understandable because you need a car to get around. But it's not worth going into debt to have a nice car while you're in residency. Stick with something basic, and if cars are important to you, you can buy a nicer one when you're making more money in the future and have given your finances a chance to catch up.

If you're about to take on new auto debt, you should be able to pay cash for whatever car you're going to buy. How much you spend on a new car should depend on whether you're a car person—is the car one of your main goals? If so, you could spend more knowing you can't spend that money on something else.

Regardless of how nice a car you choose, you should be able to buy your car for cash. And if you can't because you're still in training, then be responsible and buy something that fits into your budget, knowing the next car you buy has to be for all cash. If your car dies and you still have a loan, that puts you in a bad situation, so pay off the auto loan as quickly as you can. And if you're an attending, you need to get rid of any auto debt and know that your next car is going to be paid in cash.

MORTGAGES

Mortgages are a form of debt. But a lot of people don't think of them that way.

When I ask people if they're debt-free, I often get the answer, "Yes, except for the house." For some reason, people separate mortgages from other types of debt. Perhaps it's because they've been trained to think of a mortgage as an investment. It's not—it's a liability. It's debt. You don't want to be in debt of any kind when you retire, and a mortgage you haven't paid off could keep you from retiring when you want to.

In a later chapter, we'll help you figure out how much house you can afford so you don't end up taking on a mortgage that will cripple your finances. If you haven't bought a house yet, we'll help you figure out what you should spend. If you have bought a house, we'll help you analyze whether or not you made a good decision.

TWO WAYS TO TACKLE DEBT

Avalanche Method

With the avalanche method, you take the debt with the highest interest rate and focus on paying it off first. Pay the minimum on all of your debt except for the one with the highest interest rate. Whatever you can afford to pay in addition to those minimum payments, allocate it to the highest-interest loan. For example, if you have an extra $100 each month after paying the minimum on all your loans, that would go to your highest-interest loan.

When you've paid off the highest-interest loan, take all the money you were paying toward that loan and pay it toward the next highest. This is the mathematical approach to paying the smallest possible amount toward your loans.

Snowball Method

With the snowball method, you pay off the smallest amount of debt you have first. Say you had three loans, and their amounts were $100,000, $50,000, and $20,000. With the snowball method, you would get rid of the $20,000 loan first by paying anything extra that you can on top of the minimum payment. Once that's gone, you have the extra money you were paying toward it to put toward the $50,000 loan. This way, you stack your payments and continue to pay the same amount, but you pay the loans off faster as you go.

Mathematically, this method might not work out to be the most beneficial in the long run because it doesn't have anything to do with the interest rate—you just focus on the amount you have to pay down. But mentally and behaviorally, people like repaying their loans this way because you get a small win with each loan you pay off. You can turn it into a game and use your progress as motivation to keep going.

Let's imagine an extreme example to help you visualize why the snowball method can be more rewarding mentally. Say I have $100,000 of debt at 20% interest, and then I've got a whole bunch of little loans on top of that, at 10%. Most people would not want to keep burying money in their $100,000 debt and barely see the dent it made, even though that would work and the total amount paid would be less in the long run. Most people would rather take out all the little loans first. Emotionally, the snowball method is a better option because you can see your progress. The avalanche method is for those who are very math driven and want to pay the lowest amount of interest possible.

WHAT

Identify all of your debt and where you currently are with that debt, then organize the information in a way that will allow you to easily understand it.

WHY

Understanding your debt will help optimize your repayment method to lower the amount of interest you pay.

RESULT

Become familiar with the types of debt you have and how each one impacts your financial health so you can choose the best repayment plan for you.

To understand your debt better, begin by ranking it in order of amount and interest rate. Then decide whether the snowball or avalanche method is right for you. You'll find illustrations of the snowball and avalanche methods in the course at **financialresidency.com/freecourse**.

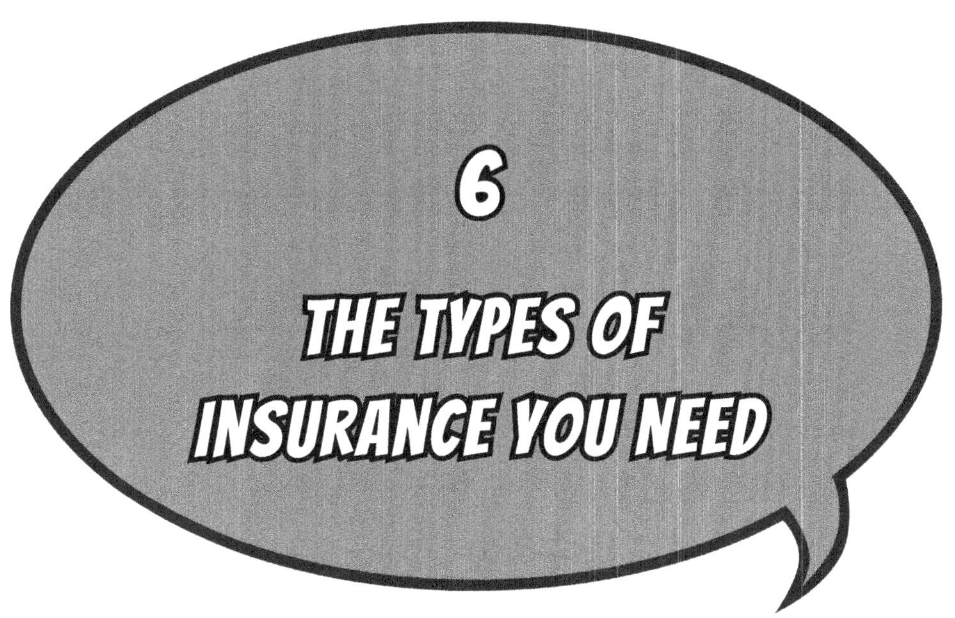

DISABILITY INSURANCE

Disability insurance is the single most important insurance you can have as a physician. One out of four Americans becomes disabled in their lifetime. What would happen to you if you became disabled and could no longer work? Do you have enough in savings to cover your expenses and maintain your lifestyle? Most physicians don't.

There are two forms of disability insurance: employer-provided and individual policies. Everyone should take advantage of their employer-provided, which will usually cover somewhere around 50-70% of your salary. It's usually capped at $5,000, $10,000, or $15,000 a month, and it's taxable. Let's say you made $10,000 in a month, and you have 50% coverage through work. That means your work will cover $5,000 of your monthly salary, and you'll be taxed on that. The part through work is taxable because you're paying with pre-tax dollars. That $5,000 might turn into $3,000 after tax. That's not enough money to live on if you were used to living on $10,000 a month.

Now you're on your own to cover the remaining portion of your salary, which is why you should get a separate policy through an independent agent. You need to cover that gap in coverage with an independent policy. Having your own disability insurance that covers you throughout your career is also beneficial if you end up as a 1099 contractor or working locum tenens for another practice. It'll be one less decision you have to make as you look for ways to grow in your career. Think of your independent disability policy as portable—wherever you go, so goes your policy.

Your individual policy "sits on top of" your employer policy. If you have a bonus pay structure, they can usually cover that, whereas your work policy typically won't cover bonus pay. There are some riders that affect how much they'll pay, such as a cost of living adjustment, a catastrophic adjustment, and others.

Statistically, women are more likely to become disabled than men, so disability insurance is more expensive for women. Similarly, men tend to die earlier than women, so term life insurance is more expensive for men. If a male and a female physician both wanted a 20-year level term life policy for $1 million, the woman may spend $300 a year while the man spends $800 a year. For a $10,000 disability insurance policy, assuming the same age/earnings/specialty, a female may pay somewhere in the ballpark of $4,000 where a male might pay $2,500.

Here's something to note for all the female physicians reading—you potentially have something of tremendous value and importance available to you. It's called a gender-neutral or a unisex rate, which is a hybrid rate for both males and females. There are a limited number of companies that offer their own occupation coverage to physicians, and an even smaller number of companies offer a unisex rate.

If it's available to you, the solution for a female physician is to purchase a policy that includes a unisex or gender-neutral rate structure along with a discount, as this could save 40-50% of the normal female premium rates.

So how do you get this unisex rate? You would normally purchase a disability policy as part of a multi-life discount, which means an employer sponsors a discount plan for employees who work for the same practice or the same hospital. You can also purchase it through a guaranteed standard issue (GSI) plan.

Many physicians go from large residency programs to small practices that don't offer great rates for disability insurance, so it's best to get the coverage while in residency. I have a client who should have paid no more than $4,500 per year for a policy, but she didn't purchase it in training. She left training and now works for a small medical center, so her cheapest policy, for less coverage, is $8,000 a year. Is this typical? No. But if you end up going to work for an employer that hasn't negotiated any discounts with the big insurance companies, it could happen.

Thinking about moving to California from another state? Look at getting your policy in place before moving, because it is most expensive to purchase disability insurance in the state of California. While age does matter in the pricing of your disability policy (maybe 2-4%), the state in which you purchase insurance matters significantly more.

Some people don't think they need disability insurance. I have clients who make $600,000 a year as a household and say, "I can use cash flow in an emergency. My wife's also a doctor." But what if something happens and you're both disabled? You will end up having no reserves and you'll be in a real bind. What are you going to do? Your employer-provided policy will pay for $4,000. Is that enough? If you have a mortgage that's more than $4,000, you'll lose your home. You need enough coverage to maintain your lifestyle.

One of my clients had good coverage and the insurance company fought her for nearly a year trying to not pay her claim. She finally got everything approved, but she had no income even *with* insurance. She had an injury from working and couldn't perform her normal tasks at work anymore. She wasn't able to use anything she learned in training to support her practice. It was a terrible situation but thankfully it had a good outcome. She was eventually able to prove the disability, and the insurance paid out.

What if you can't get disability insurance? Wing it and hope for the best? That's not a smart decision. I have type 1 diabetes and am "uninsurable" for disability insurance. We've had to plan ways to cover our expenses in case something happened to me. One of the steps we took was to increase the amount in our emergency fund. If we didn't have two streams of income plus our investments, we would have increased it even more. Better safe than sorry, especially in the case of disability.

Taylor

TERM INSURANCE

Term insurance is fairly simple to understand. You buy coverage for a fixed amount and for a certain time period. If you die inside of the terms of the policy, your beneficiary gets the amount of the coverage. If you die outside of the policy, you get nothing.

The earlier in your career you are, the more vulnerable you are. You have a high income potential but no assets and usually a ton of debt. So you need to insure your future income source for a period of time. We tell physicians to ladder their policies. As an example, say you needed $2 million in coverage for the next 30 years. Don't just buy a $2 million policy that covers 30 years. That's the most expensive way to do it as that might cost you $2,000 a year. If you ladder it by buying $1 million at 20 years and $1 million at 30, you still have coverage, but it gives your income a chance to catch up so you can start saving, investing, and paying down debt. That coverage may only cost you $1,200 a year, creating $800 of savings.

In 20 years, you likely won't need $2 million of coverage; maybe you'll only need $1 million. Maybe you'll be financially independent and you can cancel it all by then. So by having two policies for the first 20 years and then only one for the next 10, you have the same coverage but for a cheaper cost to cover the most vulnerable time in your career.

If someone is dependent on your income—kids, a spouse, or relatives—then you need term coverage. If you don't have dependents, you probably don't need term. And it's a cheap form of insurance if you're pretty healthy.

The general rule for how much coverage you need is 10 times your annual salary + your debt – any investments. So if I make $200,000 a year, I've got $500,000 in debt, and I've got $100,000 in investments, I'd need $200,000 x 10, which would be $2 million, + $500,000. The investments are still small relative to the coverage, so they wouldn't factor into the overall amount of coverage you need. So I'd need

$2.4 million, but I round up because they don't really sell insurance at $2.4 million, so I'd buy a policy for $2.5 million.

How much term coverage do you need?

_______________ Your salary x 10
_______________ + your debt
_______________ - your investments
_______________ = insurance needed

AUTO INSURANCE

Everyone knows they need auto insurance. But physicians need more auto insurance than the average person. Don't just go with the cheapest available policy.

When you're in training, you're in survival mode, so it's probably okay to just get by with the base coverage. But when you become an attending, you need to increase those limits to the maximum. As soon as something happens and someone finds out you're a physician or you're married to a physician, you'll have issues.

A client of mine got into a fender bender that resulted in no visible damage. She said something like, "My husband's at the hospital and I can't get ahold of him." All of a sudden, the other person began to say, "Oh, my neck!" and as a result, they had a potential litigation issue on their hands.

Increase your auto coverage to the maximum the insurer allows. Then shop insurance companies every couple of years because while they should be incentivized to keep your business, other companies will try and earn your business with cheaper rates.

When we moved from Las Vegas to San Diego, I shopped around for new insurance. By moving carriers and bringing all our policies over, our insurance went down 54%.

The easiest way to grow business is to keep customers, so when you're willing to put in the effort to switch companies, you'll often find better benefits elsewhere for the same or better coverage. I was able to increase my coverage and still save some money because I took the extra hour and just did it.

UMBRELLA INSURANCE

Umbrella insurance can go by a few different names, such as personal liability insurance, but it describes a policy that sits over other insurances.

As a doctor, you have a high amount of liability. You may have significant assets that need to be protected, and your risks can be higher than people in other occupations. Umbrella insurance helps protect you from gaps in your other insurance policies. It's backup insurance that kicks in after your other policies have paid out, and it covers your personal liability. That means if an accident occurs on your property or due to your actions or equipment, the umbrella insurance would cover it.

Let's look at an example. Say you own your home and something on that property caused someone to be injured—they could sue you for it, but umbrella insurance would cover what goes above your homeowners policy. If someone slips on the ice in your driveway and is injured, they could sue you. Umbrella insurance would cover medical expenses, lost wages, and emotional distress for the injured person, as well as any legal fees you incurred.

When you're shopping for umbrella insurance, you should look for a policy that covers all assets you can't afford to lose. It should cover all your properties, vehicles, boats, retirement accounts, and limited partnerships or LLCs.

WHAT

Understand your financial risks and the options available to cover those risks.

WHY

This will allow you to find the red flags and gaps in your coverage that would put you and your family in jeopardy.

RESULT

Find the coverage that will eliminate your current financial risks.

Understanding insurance policies is one of the most difficult parts of creating your financial plan. There is a huge number of products out there. In the complimentary course, you'll find a worksheet to help you better understand what you need and what you already have so you can begin filling in the gaps. Go to **financialresidency.com/freecourse**.

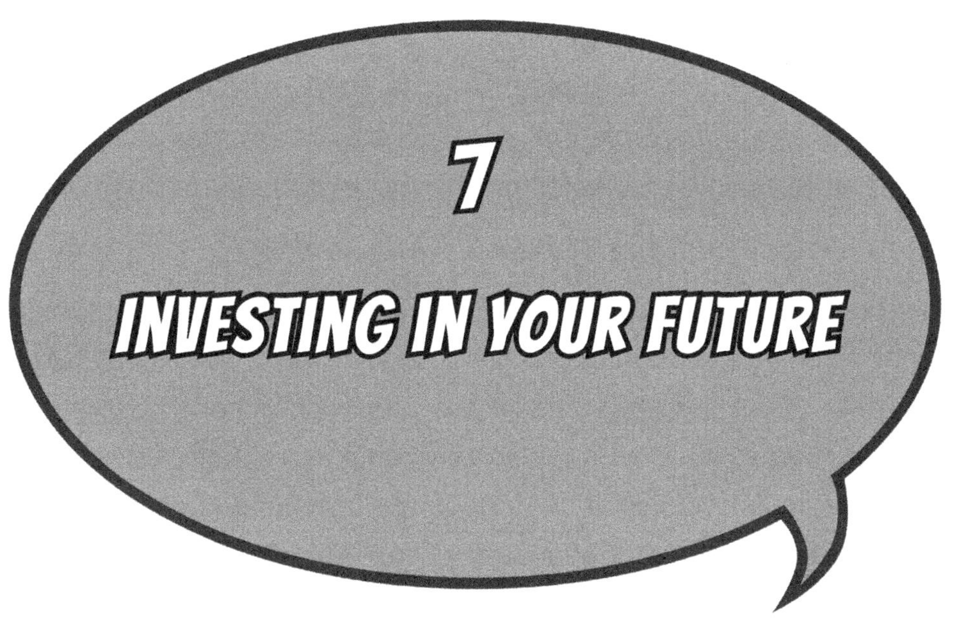

MOST COMMON RETIREMENT PLANS

You're probably already familiar with the 401(k). It's one of the most commonly known retirement plans, sponsored by private employers. The 403(b) is less well known, but in the physician world it's quite common. It's a retirement plan sponsored by certain tax-exempt companies and religious groups. Formally, it's called a tax-sheltered annuity. Just like the 401(k), 403(b) plans are made to help employees save for retirement.

You can contribute up to a certain amount toward your 401(k) or 403(b) each year. Your employer decides whether they want to match the amount or not. Usually employers match based on a percentage of your salary, although there is a cap on how much can be contributed total between you and your employer. The money your employer matches is basically free, so it's best to take advantage of their contribution to maximize your 401(k) or 403(b) contributions if that option is available to you.

Contributions to non-Roth plans like the 401(k) and 403(b) are deducted from your taxable income. That means you get a tax break up front, but you'll owe taxes on the money when you begin withdrawing it during retirement.

Unlike these non-Roth plans, with a Roth account, you contribute money that has already been taxed, so you don't have to pay taxes on it later. That means the money in your Roth account grows tax-free and comes out tax-free. Without getting into specific tax advice, because that's impossible to do in a book, most attendings should not utilize a Roth plan, because your tax rate will likely be lower in retirement than it is currently.

Some employee retirement plans require that you work for the company for a certain period of time before you're eligible. For example, your employer might state that the portion they match will vest at 100% of the contribution after three years. If you work there for three years and one day, the 100% is all yours. But if you work less than three years, the employer will typically have a scaled vesting schedule so you receive a portion of the money but not all of it.

Investing in 401(k) and 403(b) plans is still pretty limited, and it's not going to cover what you'll need in retirement. You're going to have to invest more outside of your employer plans for retirement.

DEFERRED COMPENSATION PLAN

The 457(b), also known as the deferred compensation plan, is similar to a 403(b). It's for local public employees and some nonprofit organizations and hospitals. It has similar contribution limits to a 403(b). If your employer offers both, you can contribute the maximum amount to both plans. As you put this money away, it lowers your taxable income.

Unlike the 403(b), your 457(b) stays on your employer's books as part of their general assets. The 457(b) plan is a promise by your employer to pay you the money that is deferred into the account. But if your employer filed bankruptcy and they hadn't put the 457(b) accounts in a trust, you could potentially lose a portion or all of the money, as you would become a creditor. If you work in a governmental agency, there shouldn't be a problem with bankruptcy. If you work for a private company, you may have to investigate whether the company is financially stable.

Some employers will choose to not match the contributions for a 457(b). Instead, they will open up a 401(a) to match the 457(b). For example, if you put $19,000 into your retirement account and the employer wanted to match, they would put their portion into the 401(a) instead.

INDIVIDUAL RETIREMENT ARRANGEMENTS (IRAs)

An IRA is a government-sponsored, tax-advantaged individual retirement plan. It has nothing to do with your employer.

Traditional IRA

The traditional IRA is somewhat similar to a 401(k). Your contributions lower your tax burden for the year that you make them, however, the deductibility is based on your income or your adjusted gross income and your filing status. As an attending, you will not get this deductibility as you will be phased out (because you make too much money).

As of 2019, you can't get any deductions on your contributions if you earn more than $74,000 per year if you are single, or more than $123,000 per year if you are married, filing jointly. If you're married filing separately, you can't make more than $100,000 per year.

At age 72, you are required to make withdrawals each year, called required minimum distributions (commonly referred to as RMDs). The IRS expects you to pay regular income taxes on the withdrawals. If you don't make withdrawals, you will have a 50% penalty between the amount you withdrew and the amount you should have withdrawn.

The Roth IRA

A Roth IRA works similarly to a traditional IRA, with a few differences. You do not get any tax deduction in the year you contribute, which means you have to pay tax on the money in the same tax year you put it in the Roth account. It grows tax-free (like a traditional IRA) and when you withdraw the money in retirement, it all comes out tax-free.

You need a certain income level to be eligible for the Roth IRA. That income must be earned income, and there's a contribution maximum. As an attending, you are not able to contribute directly into a Roth IRA as you make too much money to be eligible.

The Roth 401(k) doesn't have any income restrictions. If you are an attending physician, you probably shouldn't put money into a Roth 401(k) because your tax rates will likely be lower in retirement.

The Spousal IRA

If you are married and filing jointly, you can contribute to an IRA in the name of your non-working spouse if you've earned enough income. The spousal IRA works the same as a traditional IRA.

Backdoor Roth

The backdoor Roth is ***not*** a particular account but a strategy that has been acknowledged as a viable "loophole." It utilizes two accounts, a Roth IRA and a traditional IRA. Using this strategy is kind of like advanced tax planning.

If you happen to be phased out of a Roth because you have reached the income limit (meaning you make too much money and can't directly contribute to a Roth IRA), then you can make what's called a nondeductible contribution directly into a traditional IRA. If you do not have any money in any other traditional IRAs (or SEP IRAs) then the money you just contributed to the traditional IRA could be converted (moved) to a Roth IRA account that you have set up.

This would allow what would have been a nondeductible contribution into your traditional IRA (you would have received no tax benefit as you couldn't take a deduction on your taxes in the year you made the contribution) to be converted to a Roth IRA, where it would get to grow tax-free and you would be able to withdraw it tax-free in retirement.

Now, what if you have money in a traditional IRA? Are you stuck? No, you can still do this, but it will take a bit more work on your end. What you will likely want to do is transfer your traditional IRA into your employer-sponsored plan (your 401(k) or 403(b)). Once you have completed that transfer, you will end up with $0 in your traditional IRA. This will give you the green light to take advantage of the backdoor Roth strategy.

HEALTH SAVINGS ACCOUNT

HSA stands for health savings account. It's a triple tax-advantaged account. There's nothing better than that in the U.S. tax code—you get a deduction when you put money in, it grows tax-free, the money comes out tax-free if it's used on qualified medical expenses, *and* you can go back in time to cover medical-related expenses that you incurred. That means if you started your HSA on January 1, 2020, if you have any co-pays or prescriptions that you pay out of pocket, save all your receipts, because in 2039 (or whenever you are ready to be "paid back") you can pay yourself back for all those costs.

Say you've paid $150,000 in out-of-pocket medical expenses. You can pull that out of your HSA tax-free, wipe the slate clean, and pay yourself back. And that money grew tax-free the whole time.

Your HSA is a really powerful account and you'll need it as you grow older. Most people put money in the HSA to get the tax benefits, but then they take it right back out to pay for expenses. Don't do that unless you're going to have to go into credit card debt to cover the expense. You want to leave the money in there to grow tax-free for as long as possible.

To qualify for an HSA, you must be covered by a qualifying high-deductible health plan, and you can't be claimed as a dependent on anyone's tax form. It's easy to set up contributions to your HSA because most employers allow you to auto-deduct from your paycheck. If your employer doesn't, you can use an inexpensive service to do it for you.

TAXABLE ACCOUNT

When you've exhausted all your options for tax-advantaged accounts, you should look into opening a taxable account to save for retirement. Contributing to your tax-deferred and employer-sponsored plans will only take you so far. You will likely need to save money outside of those accounts to live a secure retirement.

In order to keep saving and investing, open a taxable investment account. This can be an individual or joint account (if you are married) or if you have a trust, you can open a taxable account in the name of your trust. In simple terms, think of a taxable account as a checking account that can hold stocks and bonds. My opinion is it's best to not write checks out of this account. It is an account that will allow you to keep investing for your future. Remember, this account is not tax-deferred, which means you'll owe taxes each year on your investment income.

Fees

While this book will not go into the details of building a portfolio, I do want you to be aware of the fees that your investments cost. Open up your last statement for your retirement accounts or your taxable account so we can break down what you are actually investing your money into.

Using the space below on this page, let's walk through one example of this. I highly recommend you do this with every security you own.

First, write down the account where that security is located, the name of the security, and the value of the security, in dollars. Most importantly, write down how much that security costs you. You can find this by looking at what is called the expense ratio, which should be shown. If it isn't, open up Google and type in the security's ticker symbol (usually one to five letters long) and the words "expense ratio." Usually the first result should take you to a summary page that will list out the expense ratio for the security you just entered. As a general rule, anything above 0.25% is considered expensive and you should look for cheaper options.

Where? ______________________________

Name? ______________________________

Value (in dollars)? ______________________________

Expense Ratio? ______________________________

Cost? ______________________________

Once you have the expense ratio, multiply that percentage amount by the value (in dollars) and this will tell you how much it costs to own that security.

Note: If you have a financial advisor who charges assets under management (AUM), this does ***not*** include the cost they charge to manage your money. That fee is on top of the cost the security charges as well as any trading fees the custodian may charge. (A fee-only financial planner who does not charge AUM is often much cheaper and more transparent.)

WHAT

Learn the different types of accounts that you should be taking advantage of as good investments.

WHY

Doing this will help you invest in your future, lower your taxes now, and get you closer to financial independence.

RESULT

Understand why you need to contribute to these accounts and how they impact your financial future.

For this portion of the course, it's time to audit your accounts. Begin by taking an inventory. What investments do you have? What are your expense ratios? What are you actually paying? You can repeat the exercise in this chapter for each of your investments. If you want to download a sheet that can help you track more investments, head over to the free companion course at **financialresidency.com/freecourse**.

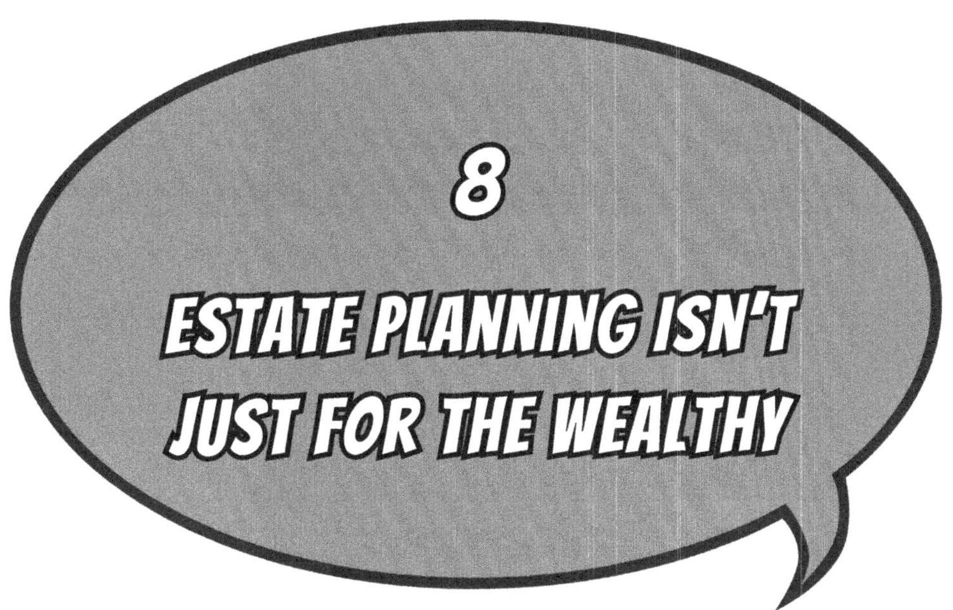

8

ESTATE PLANNING ISN'T JUST FOR THE WEALTHY

Estate planning is essential for physicians. A good estate plan will work in tandem with your financial plan and can even help pay down student debt. It's a comprehensive legal plan to protect your family, your assets, your business, and your career.

Your estate is made up of everything you own that has value in the eyes of the law, minus what you owe. Only things that have value in the eyes of the law will count toward your estate—everything else you own is simply your possessions.

That doesn't mean you can't include your possessions in your will. If you have an heirloom piano, a pet, or a collection of books that you would like to go to a particular individual or organization, you can include those items in your will. But for something to be part of your estate, it needs to have net worth in a legal sense.

Why do you need an estate plan if you're a physician? A solid estate plan will give you peace of mind and protect everything you've worked so hard to earn. Your estate plan can help you maximize your earnings to help you live a better financial life now as well as plan for the future. It will protect your assets and the people you care about, and it will protect you against unforeseen circumstances.

A good estate plan encompasses provisions for your possessions, people, and property. A solid plan will include four pillars: your will, any medical directives, a living trust, and a power of attorney.

PILLAR 1: WILL

A will is, at its simplest, a legal document that states your financial and medical wishes for after your death.

What would happen if you died without a will? Would your family be taken care of, or would they be in a financial bind without you? Who would receive the funds from your retirement plans?

The federal law states that your spouse is automatically your beneficiary. But you should still fill out the beneficiary form naming your husband or wife. If you want to name someone other than your spouse, your husband or wife will need to sign a written waiver.

No matter what you want, your wishes need to be in writing.

A scenario where that would be important is if you are separated but not yet legally divorced from your spouse and you want your money to go to someone else. Your spouse must still sign a waiver for that to happen.

Do you want your children to be beneficiaries? Money you've saved in retirement plans won't transfer directly to a minor. That means you need to appoint a trustee or guardian—again in writing—to receive and take charge of the money until the child is an adult.

In order to save time, money, and heartache, make the effort to get your beneficiaries in writing and sign the proper waivers.

ESTATE PLANNING ISN'T JUST FOR THE WEALTHY

When you die without a will—which is called intestate—your assets and debts are distributed evenly between your heirs. If you haven't named who your heirs are, the state will decide. If your heirs aren't obvious, the state may skip over anyone you may wish to benefit from your inheritance. In that case, your assets would transfer to the state. That's why it's important to name your heirs in writing.

PILLAR 2: HEALTHCARE DIRECTIVE

Every adult, not just physicians, needs a healthcare directive. You and your spouse should each complete a healthcare directive, which details your wishes and values regarding medical care in the case something happens to you and you are unable to make medical choices for yourself.

Here are some questions to consider when thinking about a healthcare directive: How far do you want a medical team to go in an attempt to save your life? In the event of a crisis, how long would you want to stay on life support? Would you consider living with a feeding tube? What are your feelings in regard to amputation? Consider your physical, mental, and spiritual needs and desires.

To create a healthcare directive, research what decisions you need to make, including the questions above. Think over and decide how you want various medical scenarios to be handled. Decide who you trust to make medical decisions for you if you are unable. Then create your advanced medical care directive and inform your family and your doctor.

Who are your choices for healthcare power of attorney?

Primary ______________________________

Secondary ______________________________

Tertiary ______________________________

PILLAR 3: LIVING TRUST

A living trust is an enforceable document crafted while you are alive, and it becomes effective after your death or if you are incapacitated. It can help you reduce estate taxes, plan care for children who are minors, ensure your family's privacy, and potentially save your adult children from themselves, so to speak, by providing limits on how they may access and use assets you leave to them.

There are two types of trusts: revocable and irrevocable. A revocable trust is exactly what it sounds like. You can revoke it—change your mind at any time. An irrevocable trust is also what it sounds like. Once you die, it stays as is. Make your decisions wisely and with legal counsel.

"Trustee" and "beneficiary" are terms that indicate the role of individuals you choose to handle your affairs, benefit from your affairs, or both.

Consider the root of each word. "Trustee" has the word "trust" as its base. The person you choose as your trustee is someone you trust to take responsibility for carrying out your wishes and respecting your choices both medically and financially.

A "beneficiary" has "benefit" as its root. This is the person or persons who benefit from the proceeds of your estate. You are the "grantor" because you have the trust. You are granting the legal right for your trustee to step in and manage your affairs if you're not able to do so. A living trust allows you to legally entrust your affairs and estate to someone you designate. You transfer your assets into the trust.

It's a good idea to give your trust a name other than your own. This is key so if you become incapacitated, your trustee technically makes decisions for the ***trust***, not for you as an individual.

This may sound silly, but it's important to fund your trust. Establishing the trust is only the first step. You must decide which assets to place in the trust and take care of the paperwork needed to move them over.

Who are your choices for trustee?

Primary ______________________________

Secondary ______________________________

Tertiary ______________________________

PILLAR 4: POWER OF ATTORNEY

The power of attorney (POA) is a document that grants the power to someone of your choice to act on your behalf for legal matters. There are multiple forms of power of attorney, which allow you to limit power to specific areas. For example, a power of attorney for asset management is limited to making decisions about your financial affairs only. Similarly, a power of attorney for healthcare appoints someone to make medical decisions for you if you don't have specific medical directives.

Who are your choices for durable power of attorney?

Primary ____

Secondary ______________________________________

Tertiary ____

ACTION STEPS

The more you have thought about your wishes, the easier it will be for you to discuss your estate plans with your attorney. Put the four pillars of estate planning into place: a will, living trust, advance care directive, and power of attorney.

You have an idea of what these four pillars do, but there are some other details you'll need to think through when putting the estate plan in place.

First, let's talk about guardians. If you have children who are minors, who will be responsible for their care should you die or become incapacitated? If they are adults, consider what, if anything, you wish to leave to them. Name a guardian for your children who are minors and decide on division of assets. If the children are minors, consider a trust to ensure your assets are professionally managed by a neutral party until your children arrive at the age you designate to receive control of the assets.

Who are your choices as guardians for your children?

Primary ______________________________

Secondary ______________________________

Tertiary ______________________________

Next up is beneficiaries. Who will receive the assets you leave behind? You can set up primary, contingent, and tertiary beneficiaries, which is a smart thing to do. Make sure this information is up to date on all of your accounts. Don't leave it up to a judge to decide where your money should go—the likelihood of your assets going where you want them to is very low in that case.

Who are the beneficiaries of your personal property?

Primary ______________________________

Secondary ______________________________

Tertiary ______________________________

Next, it's time to choose an executor. An executor is a personal representative who handles your estate once you are deceased. They ensure your wishes stated in your estate plan are carried out. This person does not need to be an attorney or legal expert. Your executor can be anyone you wish. It's best to choose a person who knows you well and whom you trust to put your best interests and personal wishes first.

Who are the executors of your estate?

Primary ______________________________

Secondary ______________________________

Tertiary ______________________________

Lastly, there are a few other important pieces of information you will need to consider.

- ❑ Do you have any family mementos or heirlooms that should go to specific people? Create a separate list for these.
- ❑ Do you have any special bequests?
- ❑ Do you have a safe deposit box?
- ❑ Do you want to include age-based distributions? (A trust will be required for this.)
- ❑ Have you entered any pre- or post-nuptial agreements?
- ❑ Is there anyone you wish to disinherit?

A DIGITAL ESTATE PLAN

Digital estate planning is the process of organizing your digital monetary and sentimental assets and making formalized arrangements for what should happen to that property and information after your death.

If you have computing hardware—and we know you do—keep a record of where your information is stored and how to access it. That record needs to be in a secure location, accessible only by your designee, to protect your privacy and your valuables.

Here is a short list of items to consider adding to your digital estate. You will need to customize the list to suit your needs, but this will get you started.

Type of Item	Stored Electronically	Stored Physically	Password Required
Credit card accounts	Yes		Yes
Credit card rewards/ points programs	Yes		Yes
Email account - personal	Yes		Yes
Email account - business	Yes		Yes
eBooks	Yes	Yes (on device)	Yes
Flash drives		Yes	No
Music	Yes	Possibly	Yes, if stored electronically
Online store accounts that you run (e.g., Etsy or eBay)	Yes		Yes
Online subscriptions to magazines, websites, apps, etc.	Yes		Yes
Retail and shopping accounts (i.e., clothing stores & grocery stores)	Yes	Yes (key tag/ barcode)	Phone number

WHAT

A comprehensive legal plan to protect your earnings, your business, your assets, and your career will help you sleep better at night in the long run.

WHY

Having a solid plan for your estate will provide peace of mind.

RESULT

An estate plan will help ensure that your hard-earned assets (and you do have assets, despite the student loan debt) are protected throughout your life and career.

It's time to craft your own estate plan. You can use the illustrations in this chapter to create a summary for your estate plan or, if you want to do it more efficiently, a template is available to download in the course. Go to **financialresidency.com/freecourse**.

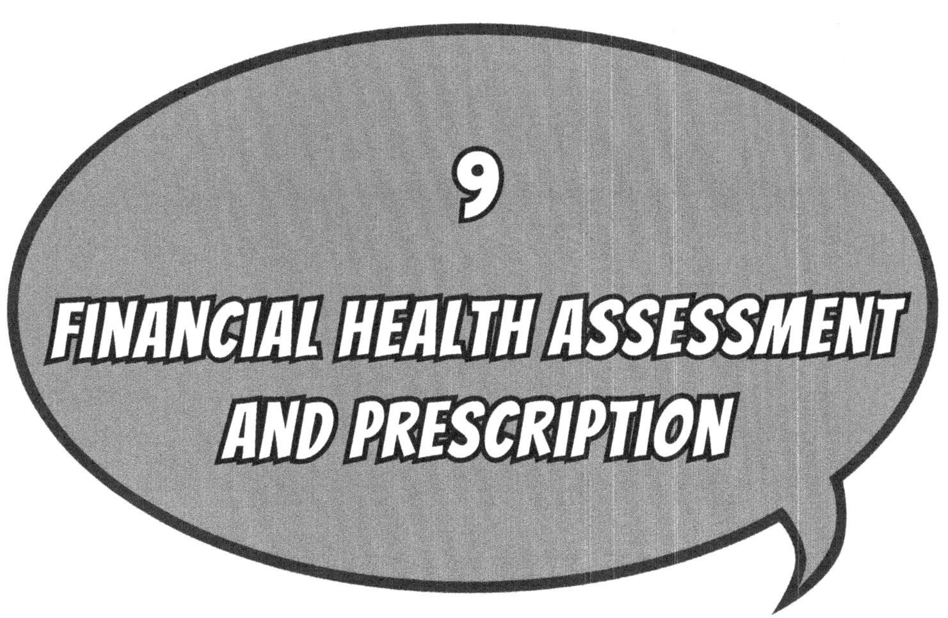

You're now ready to begin implementing the things you've learned throughout this book. You already have everything you need to begin taking action on your finances because (hopefully) you completed the exercises.

But before you move on there are four critical things you need to address, which we'll cover in this chapter. If you do nothing else, do these four things. Without them, something could go wrong and all your financial planning would be for nothing.

Once you've completed the four items below, we'll address how to implement what you've learned from previous chapters to create a complete financial plan.

1. WHEN AND WHERE TO BUY DISABILITY INSURANCE

Disability insurance is likely the most important product you can buy. Before you do anything else, take the time to research and purchase a disability policy.

There are many riders that you can put on your disability policy, but there are four major riders I deem critical to covering the biggest risks you might face: true own occupation, partial disability benefit, future purchase option (FPO), and cost of living adjustment (COLA).

True own occupation of total disability is the best type of total disability rider available in the marketplace.

A partial or residual disability rider is necessary so you will still receive a payout even if you can still work, but not to the extent you could prior to your disability.

A cost of living adjustment is a rider that adjusts the payout for your disability based on the consumer price index (CPI) or a fixed percentage.

The future increase option is a rider that gives you the option to purchase additional coverage when your need for insurance coverage increases. Your income is continually increasing and you will need to increase your coverage to match. The advantage to having this rider is you will receive more coverage throughout the years without having to undergo the underwriting process from the insurance carrier.

The disability policy you buy should be in addition to your employer-provided policy. When you're shopping for disability insurance, choose an independent provider and don't buy from anyone who uses fear as a selling tactic.

If you want to run a disability quote, go to financialresidency.com/disabilityquote.

2. TRULY UNDERSTAND YOUR STUDENT DEBT

When deciding how to handle your student debt, the first step is to decide whether or not you're going for PSLF. If your student debt exceeds two times your expected salary, then PSLF is a good idea. If you are a resident, sign up for an income-driven repayment plan and begin making payments if you haven't already, so you can reach the required 120 payments faster. Do not go into forbearance during training.

If you're not going for PSLF, take the time to learn about repayment plans and choose the one that's best for you. The goal is to pay it off within five to seven years.

If you don't know which repayment plan you should be on, check out Loan Buddy. It's a free tool I created to help you choose a repayment plan. You can access it at financialresidency.com/loanbuddy.

Remember, student debt is like buying a business and it's usually necessary to go into debt to become a physician. If you've been careful about how much debt you've taken on, you should be able to pay it off a few years after residency (if you aren't going for PSLF). The key is to continue to live a frugal life, similar to the way you did in residency, for the first five years after training. During that time, put a large portion of your new extra income toward your debt until your loans are paid off. You can begin to inflate your lifestyle to some extent at that point, but not before.

> A good rule of thumb new attendings should live by is to give themselves a 50% raise and use the rest of their income to pay down debt and invest. So if you were making $60,000 a year as a resident, raise your income to $90,000, and use whatever is left over to pay down debt or invest. If you are unsure whether you should pay down debt or invest, the flowchart in chapter 11 will help you.

3. ELIMINATE CONSUMER DEBT

What types of debt do you have, and how much of each? Which loans are necessary debt (good debt) versus unnecessary debt (bad debt)? Rank your debt and choose a method to begin attacking it. I tend to like the mathematical approach, so I prefer the avalanche method, but if you need to make smaller wins along the way to keep yourself motivated, the snowball method may be best for you.

Now that you understand the difference between good and bad debt, don't take on any unnecessary consumer debt. This kind of debt tends to have the highest interest rates, so you should pay it off as quickly as you can. If you do have to take on more consumer debt while you're in residency, create a plan to pay it off and don't fall into the trap of the monthly payment mindset. If you can't pay for something in all cash, then you cannot afford it.

4. INCREASE AUTO COVERAGE AND HAVE AN UMBRELLA POLICY

Increasing your auto insurance and purchasing an umbrella policy are relatively cheap ways to improve your financial security. It's such an oversight that many physicians don't do these things. As a physician, you can become a target for insurance fraud because people know you have a high income, and you may have a lot of assets to protect.

If you haven't switched auto insurance providers in a while, shop around to see if you can get a better price than what you're currently paying, and increase your coverage to the maximum allowed amount. Also shop for an umbrella policy to cover personal liabilities, including your properties, vehicles, businesses, and all other assets you can cover. Umbrella coverage is one of the cheapest forms of insurance for the amount of coverage provided. Coverage of $1 million dollars in umbrella insurance is likely to cost roughly $300 per year.

NEXT PRIORITIES

Once you've done the four things above, you're ready to bring your whole plan together. Don't move on until you've completed the four items above, because if those things are not in place, the rest of your financial plan may not even matter.

Based on the exercises you've completed throughout the book, you now have an outline of the pillars of finance. It's time to bring everything together to create your financial plan. Follow the flowchart below to ensure you take care of everything in order of importance, starting by creating a cash flow plan.

Now that your financial plan is taking shape, you can see the light at the end of the tunnel—the hard work is done. Everything comes back to your goals. What are you trying to accomplish? Why are you getting up and going to work every day? Everything in your financial plan should match your vision for what you want to do with your life.

STEP-BY-STEP FINANCIAL PRIORITIES

Step 1: Become Financially Solvent

- You're current on all of your debt payments and all of your expenses are paid but $0 goes toward savings.
- Asset Protection: You have health insurance, car insurance, and homeowners or renters insurance.

Step 2: Financial Stability and Paying Off Debt

- All expenses are paid each month, with a positive cash flow to build an emergency fund and pay off high interest consumer debt or personal loans.
- Asset Protection: Add disability insurance and life insurance.

Step 3: Savings and Debt Freedom

- You've paid off high interest debts, all expenses are paid each month, you have positive cash flow, and have three months of expenses saved in an emergency fund.
- Asset Protection: Add umbrella insurance.

Step 4: Financial Security and Wealth Building

- Appreciate asset accumulation by maxing out employer retirement accounts and other types of traditional investments. Work to build long-term savings to cover your future annual expenses in retirement.
- Asset Protection: Begin creating estate documents (will, medical POA (power of attorney), and health POA).

Step 5: Enhancing Life and Financial Independence

- Save beyond your needs in 529 accounts, donor-advised funds (donor-advised funds, or DAFs, provide a simple way to donate money for tax benefit purposes without specifying the beneficiary), and other "non-traditional" investments to build additional investment income.

- Asset Protection: Continue creating estate documents (living trust).

Step 6: Financial Abundance and Legacy

- Accumulate more savings than you will ever need.
- Asset Protection: Create a family foundation and irrevocable living trust.

CREATE A NET WORTH STATEMENT

A net worth statement is really easy to create. It's a single page that lists your assets and liabilities, which you've already started to list in chapter 3. This is a way for you to track net worth. Starting out, keep track of your net worth as a whole and don't worry about your investments individually or what the markets are doing. You can't control how the market ebbs and flows, but what you can control is your savings rate, how you handle your finances, and the mindset through which you view money.

Your net worth statement is like a scorecard you keep to see how you're doing financially. It should improve and your net worth should grow consistently. Your assets include stocks and bonds, bank accounts, and investments. Your liabilities are your student and car loans, consumer debt, mortgage, and any other forms of debt.

Track your net worth at least quarterly (every three months) so you have a baseline to establish where you're at and what's happening. Just like in patient care, you have to understand what's normal for the patient, so you have to track the same things with your finances.

As your net worth increases, you get closer to becoming financially independent. The goal is to create enough net worth so you can live off your assets and no longer have to work. The faster you're able to create positive net worth and build your assets, the sooner you will be able to retire.

But in order to get to that place, you need to understand the target. What's normal, where are you now, and where do you want to be? What is realistic for you to accomplish?

When you have all of your assets and liabilities written down, subtract the liabilities from the assets. If you have $100,000 of assets and $60,000 of liabilities, that would mean your net worth is $40,000.

Use this template to get started. A full-sized, editable version is located in the free companion course.

What You Own

Checking ______________________

Savings ______________________

401(k) ______________________

IRA ______________________

Other Investments ______________________

Home ______________________

529 ______________________

Business ______________________

Total ______________________

What You Owe

Mortgage ______________________

Auto ______________________

Student Loan ______________________

Consumer Debt ______________________

Business Loan ______________________

Other ______________________

Total ______________________

What You're Worth

What You Own - What You Owe = What You're Worth

______________ - ______________ = ______________

WHAT

Bring all of your financial assets and liabilities together and take care of the four things every individual must address first in their financial plan.

WHY

You're creating a financial plan that's unique to you and will help you feel more empowered to take control over your finances.

RESULT

You will have a plan that describes where you currently are and provides a prescription for how to get where you want to be.

Take the next step in your financial plan by creating a net worth statement. The exercise in this chapter gives you a template, so all you have to do is plug in the numbers from the other worksheets you've completed throughout this book. You can find a larger version of the template at **financialresidency.com/freecourse**.

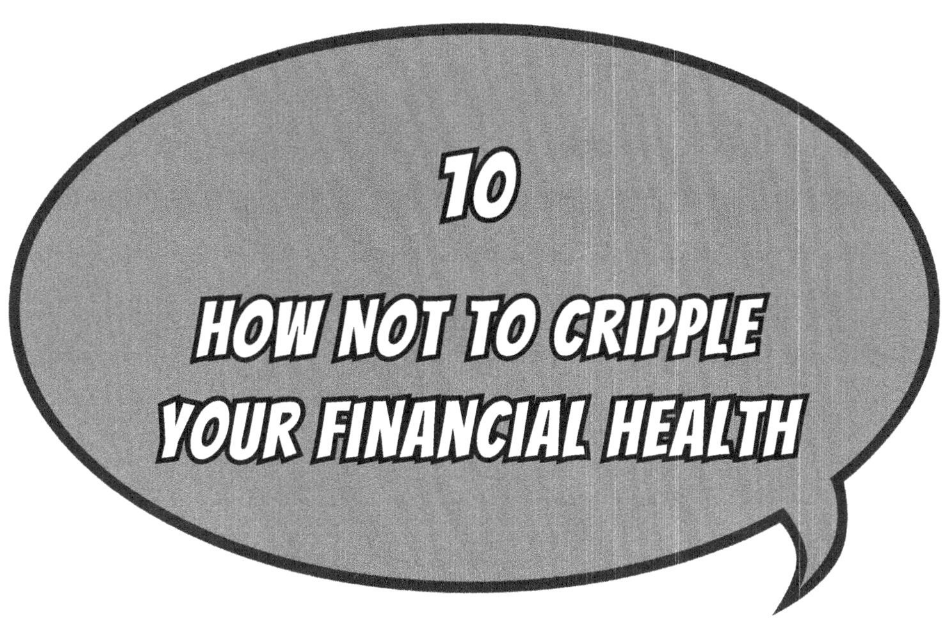

There are four things that can cripple your financial health. You want to avoid all of these things. Be honest with yourself as you read these mistakes—is there something you need to change about the way you handle money?

THE MONTHLY PAYMENT MINDSET

A lot of physicians fall into the monthly payment mindset. They think they can afford whatever they want if they can afford the monthly payment, and they end up living paycheck to paycheck because of it. They don't stop to think about how much something truly costs because it's hard to see when it's divided into small monthly portions.

While you should plan your cash flow based on your monthly spending, you cannot think about the affordability of anything in terms of monthly payments. Yes, you can afford a $1,500-a-month car payment because you make a good salary. But if you can't afford the $90,000 the car costs in cash, you can't afford the car, because that car really costs $110,000 after you've paid it off.

You may think that 0% interest is no problem, and you can justify a monthly payment that way. Sure, it may not cost any more than if you paid in cash, but it's a psychological trick, and you need to be aware of it. You may tell yourself, "I can buy this piece of furniture for $1,000; I only have to pay $25 a month and it's no interest." If you actually needed that piece of furniture, that would be a fine way to pay for it. But you may see that easy $25-a-month payment and think it's no big deal. You might say, "It's not going to cost anything. I can afford $25 a month. Why not buy it?" And then you end up buying something you don't actually need or, worse, spending money on something that ultimately doesn't make you happier.

Similarly, the majority of people get tricked into buying things because they're on sale. Say the sale is buy two get one free, and you only needed one, but you bought two because you got a third free. Now you have two that you didn't need, and you paid twice as much as you should have. Don't fall for these types of marketing ploys.

BECOMING AN OSTRICH

Don't shove your head in the sand and hope everything will work out, thinking you'll deal with your finances at a later date. This will especially hurt you if you have student debt. Pay attention. You have to make an effort to educate yourself. Shoving your head in the sand and pretending that everything will work out might cost you hundreds of thousands of dollars. Take some ownership and responsibility for your finances. Personal finance may seem daunting, but it really isn't when you break it up piece by piece.

LIFESTYLE INFLATION

Many physicians allow their lifestyle to inflate with their income. They make purchases they can't afford. They have a high income, so they allow their lifestyles to match that income despite having large amounts of debt.

We all find ways to spend money when it's there if we don't allocate it to something. Letting your lifestyle inflate is probably the single greatest destroyer when physicians don't pay attention to their finances, like an ostrich with its head in the sand. Those two habits combined can devastate people who are making $600-700,000 a year. Even on that salary, they can live paycheck to paycheck because they aren't paying attention to their finances and they're living a lifestyle above what they can actually afford.

The true problem is when lifestyle inflation is not controlled. It can hinder your ability to live your ideal life because you're not spending your money on what's most important to you. It begins with a purchase here and a purchase there. It turns into needing a better car, a bigger house, or a more luxurious vacation. Eventually you begin to feel that the moment your paycheck hits your account it's already spent on something—usually fixed monthly payments.

Before making a purchase, take a moment and ask yourself these simple questions, and you'll be saving money in no time.

1. Why do I want this new thing?
2. Am I buying it to make me feel better?
3. Is this something I truly need?

I frequently get asked, "How do I place boundaries on my wants and needs?" First, you have to recognize that wants and needs are very different things.

To begin creating boundaries, start by answering these three questions.

Why do you feel you are not living the lifestyle you want?

Why do you feel your current lifestyle is not good enough?

What is an area of your life that needs more attention?

Next, create a list of your wants and needs, then put a price tag next to each of them. What will each of them cost you?

Wants	**Needs**
________________	________________
________________	________________
________________	________________
________________	________________

Now let's add each of those needs into your cash flow plan. Adjust what you think you will spend in each area of the cash flow plan and see how it affects your savings rate. Are you able to hit the 25% savings rate and still get in all your needs? What if you add in all your wants and recalculate—will you still hit the savings goal?

It is likely that you won't, and that's okay. In fact, it's totally ***normal***.

That means you will need to go through your entire cash flow plan and prioritize what the first cash out of your account goes toward. Normally I'd coach clients to start with 25% of their income going into savings to pay themselves first, and then use the other 75% to live however they want. Of course student debt, childcare, housing, and food are all secured at the top of the list, but where does everything else shake out?

Keep listing your spending priorities until you run out of money to allocate. Do a review of everything that didn't make the cut—is there anything on that list that brings you more happiness than something that did make the list of priorities? If so, reprioritize the list until you are comfortable with what you have. This is a shortcut to start designing the life you want to live. Be the true CFO of your household. Tell your money how you want it to work in order to make you, the boss, happy.

Remember, it will be a trade-off. Spending more money on a larger mortgage means you'll have less money to spend on discretionary expenses like dining out. Which provides more happiness: dining out frequently or having a bigger home? I can't answer that for you. No one can but you. But it's a decision you need to make, and the more informed you are, the higher the likelihood you'll live your ideal life.

THINKING INSURANCE IS AN INVESTMENT

There are many complex insurance products out there, such as whole life or universal life insurance. ***Those products are designed to be sold, not bought.*** The people selling them make a ton of money and there's almost always a better way to save or invest than to buy that type of product. They're sold as an investment, but they're not.

Insurance is insurance and investments are investments. Never mix the two.

Insurance agents will tell you insurance is an investment. "You can access the cash inside this at any time and give yourself a loan." They fail to tell you the high fees that are associated with it.

They make you think you're saving your money somewhere. But if you try to get your money out in the first eight to 10 years, it's likely there will be less money than you first put in. That is one of the worst investments you could have in that short period of time. Agents can make the time argument, that it'll be more valuable later, but if you were to just invest that money for eight to 10 years—not in insurance—you would come out ahead.

Remember, they're selling insurance. It's not an investment product, but they phrase it like it's an investment. They'll say, "You're saving for your future." They often won't tell you there's usually a ceiling on how much you can make. There's a participation rate, which varies by the product and the company selling you the insurance.

Let's say you can participate at up to 12%. That means the market can increase 100% and the most you'll get is 12%. The insurance company keeps the rest. They're taking on the risk and exposure, so they need to limit you somehow. They do it through fees and capping.

WHAT

These common mistakes would implode your finances and set you back several years or cost you hundreds of thousands of dollars.

WHY

Identifying these mistakes can help you understand how they could be impacting your financial health.

RESULT

If you don't make these mistakes, you will remove the obstacles throughout your financial journey.

I'm often asked whether it's best to prioritize paying off debt or to invest the money instead. Below is a list of steps that will set you up for stability if you follow them in order to invest and pay off your debt.

1. Contribute to your 401(k)/403(b) up to the match your employer provides.

2. Pay off any high interest debt (8% and higher).

3. Create an emergency savings fund (one month of current expenses).

4. Contribute to your Health Savings Account ($3,550 single and $7,100 married in 2020).

5. Max out your Roth IRA if eligible ($6,000/person/year in 2020).

6. Max out the remainder of your 401(k)/403(b) ($19,500/person/year in 2020).

7. Utilize backdoor Roth contributions if you're not eligible for a Roth IRA ($6,000/person/year in 2020).

8. Fill up emergency savings to have three months of total expenses a minimum.

9. Pay down any debt that is between 5-8% interest rate.

10. Contribute to a taxable investment account.

11. Pay down any debt with an interest rate less than 5%.

Steps 10 and 11 can be reversed or split—there's no right or wrong answer here. If you made it to that point, great work!

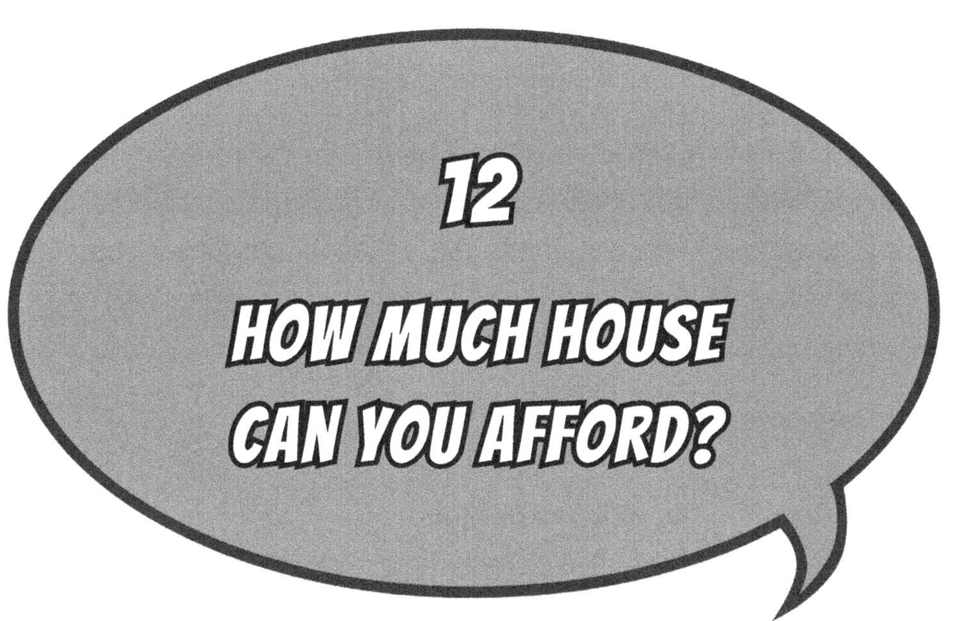

12 HOW MUCH HOUSE CAN YOU AFFORD?

Below are some guidelines to help you determine how much house you can afford. Make buying a home a reality using the calculations we've provided to find the maximum amount you can spend on a house. Asking a bank how much they'll loan to you is not a good way to assess what you can afford.

1. Consider how much you're bringing in.

Add up all of your take-home pay—the money that hits your bank account each month. This is the first data point we will need in our calculation. For this example, let's say your monthly pay is $12,000.

Take-home pay: ____________________

2. Multiply your take-home pay by 25%.

By multiplying your take-home pay by 25%, you will get the maximum amount you can afford to spend monthly on your home. This is not your maximum mortgage payment. It is the amount you can pay toward your mortgage payment plus all of the other expenses. Those expenses would be principle, interest, taxes, insurance, HOA dues, maintenance and repairs, utilities, etc. For example, $12,000 x 25% = $3,000.

Take-home pay x 25% = ____________________

3. Determine the extra expenses.

In the next step, we will determine principle, interest, taxes, and insurance (PITI). But before we get there, you need to determine what all your extra expenses are. Add up your HOA dues, any special assessments (such as additional property tax), and budget for deferred maintenance and repairs. With our example, we will use $500 a month as the total cost for these extra expenses.

Extra expenses:

____

____

____

____

Total = ____________________

4. Use the mortgage calculator to determine your maximum mortgage payment.

Now that we have determined the maximum amount you can afford to allocate in your budget to a home purchase (step 2), subtract the additional expenses from that number (as calculated in step 3) to determine the maximum mortgage payment you can afford each month.

Here is an example to see how we work through it:

- $450,000 purchase price and loan amount at 3.75%
- $4,500 property tax (1% of purchase price), 0% down payment
- $600-per-year homeowners insurance

This will bring the monthly mortgage amount that you can realistically afford to $2,500.

So, how much home will that buy?

If your take-home pay is $12,000 a month, that means the maximum amount you can allocate for a home is $3,000 a month (as calculated in step 2). If you have an additional $500 a month of extra expenses (as calculated in step 3), then you can afford a $450,000 home as shown above.

If you want to purchase a home that is more expensive, you will need to have a down payment to keep the monthly payment the same. For example, if the home is $500,000 and you keep everything else the same, you will need a $50,000 down payment.

Use the mortgage calculator at financialresidency.com/affordcalculator to determine your maximum mortgage payment. You will likely need to play around a bit to get to the maximum mortgage payment you calculated already by adjusting the loan amount in the calculator.

For all the amazing information available at Financial Residency, go to FinancialResidency.com. For more information on the topics covered in this book, follow the links below.

Financial Residency

- financialresidency.com/start-here

Getting Organized

- financialresidency.com/organized-financial-life

Budgeting

- financialresidency.com/5-steps-to-create-a-budget-worth-using

Student Debt

- financialresidency.com/studentloan
- financialresidency.com/podcast/pay-off-debt-or-invest

Mortgage

- financialresidency.com/physician-mortgage-loans
- financialresidency.com/affordcalculator

Insurance

- financialresidency.com/comprehensive-guide-to-disability-insurance-what-every-physician-needs-to-know
- financialresidency.com/disabilityquote

Investing

- financialresidency.com/investing

If this book overwhelms you and you have no interest in finance, by all means, hire a fee-only financial planner to get you on the right track. Just don't stick your head in the sand and hope that it all works out. Either way, you need to be aware of what's going on with your finances so you can make sure your financial plan is aligned with your goals. This book will give you the understanding you need to make the financial decisions that are best for you.

Physician Wealth Services
PhysicianWealthServices.com

Physician Wealth Services (PWS) is a fee-only financial planning practice helping physician families take control of their finances to position themselves for a bright financial future. We help physicians sleep well at night knowing they have a trusted advisor who is guiding them toward financial independence. Our goal is to take care of you while you take care of your patients. We are accessible when you are—in the evenings after you get your kids to bed, during your commute home, or between patients. Short of the overnight shift, consider us on call. Most importantly, we are fiduciaries for our clients and we work exclusively with physicians all around the country.

For more information, go to PhysicianWealthServices.com

Financial Fellowship (membership site)
FinancialFellowship.com

Financial Fellowship is a do-it-yourself way to build a financial plan that combines the brainpower and forces of a physician/physician-family membership community. The goal is that in one year, you will have built your custom financial plan, unique to you and what you want to achieve, with comprehensive tools and the support and accountability of the community to get it done. Two years after joining this membership, you'll be living a financial plan that was created and implemented by you.

For more information, go to FinancialFellowship.com

***Financial Residency* Podcast**
financialresidency.com/podcast

You spent decades in school to get to where you are as a doctor, but during medical school and residency, you probably didn't receive an education dedicated to your finances. Don't worry, that's where the podcast comes in. Think of it as your financial residency without the long hours and sleepless nights. You'll understand how you make money, how you spend money, how your hard-earned money can work for you, and how to protect yourself and your family. It's okay to not know the difference between a Roth IRA and a 403(b) or know which 529 plan is best. I will simplify highly complex concepts and translate industry jargon into plain English. Are you ready to take action and make smarter, more informed financial decisions? Great—let's do this! Let your financial residency begin. Find us on all the major podcast players: Apple, Stitcher, iHeart Radio, Spotify, Google, and more!

FB Group: www.facebook.com/groups/physicianfinance

Twitter: @physicianwealth

Instagram: www.instagram.com/financialresidency

Ryan Inman is the host of the *Financial Residency* podcast and President of Physician Wealth Services, a fee-only financial planning firm that works exclusively with physicians across the country. He helps physicians create a life they love using the resources they have. This helps them feel more in control of their money in the same way a physician makes a patient feel better about their health.

Taylor Inman, M.D., Ryan's better half, is a pediatric pulmonologist at Naval Medical Center San Diego. She received her medical degree from the University of Kansas School of Medicine and did pediatrics training at CHOC Children's in Orange, California, and a pediatric pulmonologist fellowship. She believes physicians have the power within to create and pursue their ideal lives and, with the right balance and determination, they can do just about anything—making them the ultimate superheroes.

Made in the USA
Las Vegas, NV
07 May 2021